Visitors To My Street

1940's and 1950's

BERNARD T. McCANN

outskirts
press

Visitors To My Street
1940's and 1950's
All Rights Reserved.
Copyright © 2022 Bernard T. McCann
v5.0

The opinions expressed in this manuscript are solely the opinions of the author and do not represent the opinions or thoughts of the publisher. The author has represented and warranted full ownership and/or legal right to publish all the materials in this book.

This book may not be reproduced, transmitted, or stored in whole or in part by any means, including graphic, electronic, or mechanical without the express written consent of the publisher except in the case of brief quotations embodied in critical articles and reviews.

Outskirts Press, Inc.
http://www.outskirtspress.com

Paperback ISBN: 978-1-9772-5126-8
Hardback ISBN: 978-1-9772-5189-3

Library of Congress Control Number: 2022901209

Cover Photo © 2022 Bernard T. McCann. All rights reserved - used with permission.

Outskirts Press and the "OP" logo are trademarks belonging to Outskirts Press, Inc.

PRINTED IN THE UNITED STATES OF AMERICA

This book is dedicated to my brother Francis McCann, who passed away this year, before the completion of this work. He alone shared with me the experiences of much of what is described in this book. His inspiration and encouragement kept me moving forward with this project.

My brother and my protector, holding me

Table of Contents

Prologue i
Note to the Reader v
The People of the Neighborhood and Visitors to the Street ... 1
Uncle's Return After the War 9
Brigid Hanley 16
Return to Plattsburgh for Mom 18
In Car Games 21
In the Greater World 22
Front Porches 22
Mystery Solved 30
Milk Right to Your Home 31
Bakery Deliveries 32
Fresh Eggs 33
The Insurance Man 33
Bees 34
Neighborhood Mailman 34
The Basilica and Father Baker 35
Sounds of the Plant 39
Constant Train Traffic 39
Infants Out for a Walk 40
"Rags – Ragideh" 40
Get Your Fresh Vegetables 42

Transportation	42
Get Your Knives Sharpened	43
Fuller Brush Man	43
Workers at the Plant	44
Ice	45
Garbage	45
Coal	46
Television	47
Radio	49
Street Name Origins	50
The Hanley Family	51
Death of a Giant	52
Dad's Love of Sports	53
Victory Gardens	55
Canning and Sister Kathleen	56
Picking Peaches	57
Sister Kathleen's Twenty-fifth Anniversary as a Nun	58
Loretta Kraft	60
Thunderstorms	62
My World Expands	63
Mom's Death	66
Clean Floors	74
Local Dairy	75
Leaves	75
Sledding	76
Hydraulic Engineers	78
Love of Flowers	78
Roller-skating	79
Go Fly a Kite	79
The Attic	80
Chestnut Ridge Picnics	81
Football	82

Mothers on the Street	84
Ross Guarino, Sr.	85
The Women of Colton	85
Family Vacation in Canada	87
Tea and Toast and Holy Communion	89
Early Childhood Education	90
Dad's Night School	92
Francis "Kelly" McCann	92
Back to Colton	93
Family Gatherings	94
Winter Afternoon Light	99
Bus Ride to Downtown Buffalo	99
Outdoor Market at Clinton and Bailey	110
Piano Lessons	111
Corning New York	113
The OLV Environs	116
Very Important People	117
Going to School at OLV	122
The School Playground	124
Victory Playground	128
Street Dances	131
The Drug Store	131
Caretaker of the Community	132
Neighborhood Gathering	133
Mom's Best Friend	134
Why People Were So Close	137
The Bat	138
Crystal Beach	139
Riding a Bike	142
Lent and Easter Season	143
Holy Thursday and Good Friday	145
Saturday Afternoon Movies	146

Shoes	147
My Radio	148
Bob Barrett	149
Mom's Daily Routine	150
Frances Guarino	151
Grandmother Moran	152
Yearly Visitors to School	154
World Events Invade Our House	155
The Paperboy	155
First Job	156
Bridges	158
Jim's Corner Store	160
Niagara Falls	161
Our "Happy Days"	162
Haircuts	163
Mike Osborne	164
Sunday Night Hide and Seek	165
Parks Galore	166
The Merricks	168
Botanical Gardens	169
Ann Austin	171
Korean War	173
To School with Mom	174
Scouts	175
Sports	176
Ridge Road Businesses	178
My Cousin Bernard McDonnell	179
The Langans	184
Lawyer Sullivan	184
My Bike	185
The Trip Mom Did Not Get to Take	185
First Trip to Washington DC	187

Lonely Summers	190
My Lost Bike	191
At the Old Knights of Columbus	192
Who Am I?	193
Local library	193
Train Station	194
Chestnut Ridge Park	195
Dad at the Beach	197
Travel by Wagon	197
Trips to the Dentist	198
As My World Expanded New Experiences	199
War Games	200
Other Uses for Baseball Cards	200
Street Coverings Changed our Games	201
Ring-a-Levio	201
Confession	202
The Plant	203
The Report Card	204
Memorial Day	205
Ice Machine	206
Roller Skating Colton and Victory	206
Fireflies	207
Summer Ritual	208
Gift for Dad one Christmas	208
Sad Story	209
A special visitor to the neighborhood	215
Epilogue	216
Special Thanks	218

Prologue

Memory is a wonderful, but fickle mechanism, when it attempts to bring back reflections of places and of people long departed. Time is a great influencer on how well those memories mirror the actual people, and events. Scope also effects your memory. My scope was limited to our neighborhood where everything and everyone was safe and protective of one another. Now in my seventy-seventh and seventy-eighth year, I am trying to reach back through time and put words to the images in my mind of what life was like in the mid to late 1940's and into the 1950's. The period is from my first memories to starting high school. I leave to those few who can share the memory of those times and places how accurate I have been. For those who did not share that time, you will have to take my word for it.

When the reader completes this book, they will have shared, in the detail of a life, for a small boy in a steel mill town, in upstate New York. That time was as complex as we have always been afraid to admit. Life and death were as real as now. Radio was king but TV was soon to amaze us. There will be reflected a closeness between neighbors that no longer dominates the American scene. It was a time when children strove to be bigger than they had a right to be. It was a time of hope in the post war era. It was a time when people collectively sighed with relief after having lived through the Depression and then World War Two.

The small boy will experience pain, death, and happiness and love. When questions became unanswerable, he had two places to go, one is a magnificent church with an Altar to God, and the other was a small creek where under a bridge he could be all alone with himself and his thoughts.

There is so much I remember about that small boy who is now wandering around in the memory of an old man. Hopefully, those remembered people and places will be drawn from my recollection and into your consciousness.

Speaking of memory, mine is still valid these days. It goes all the way back to when I was four years old. That memory is illuminated with bright yellow sunshine, dappled with the green reflective leaves of large Elm and Maple trees that graced Colton Avenue, like stationary guardians in front of each house.

The reality was that steel dust covered everything. At home, the windowsills had to be dusted every day in the warm weather. In the wintry weather, snow was always a light gray color.

Generally, it was a quiet neighborhood, because all the dads were at work and the older children were in school. There were few cars on the street in the immediate aftermath of World War Two. Only the moms were around, but their days were so filled with doing the wash, hanging it out to dry on clotheslines held up by spear like clothes poles and cleaning house and preparing dinner that we saw little of them during the day. My mom worked, so my grandmother, who lived with us, was the constant presence. If I was home for lunch and dinner, she was happy.

The war was just over, my uncles returned (2) and all my first cousin's (7) returned home safely as well and the world, at least mine, was at peace.

The idea for this book took root back in 1992 when I first made an outline. I did very little about actually writing until 2019.

Mom holding me in the summer of 1946. (This photo would be included in the 1952 Lackawanna High School Yearbook as a memorial to my mom}

Note to the Reader

The book is not set up in any order. I have inserted topic headings, so you know the theme of each section. I digress from the themes quite often and for that I apologize. However, one story bleeds into another and just seems to fit at that moment. The world was/is a changing place in so many ways. I try to depict those changes, such as, the transition from radio to television, close knit neighborhoods to housing developments, where few neighbors know each other, from kids playing outdoors using their imaginations and entertaining themselves to kids glued to screens on phones and computers. I hope you enjoy this journey back in time. This is a but snapshot of life for me and people from the forties and fifties.

Map of the immediate area of the Colton neighborhood in Lackawanna

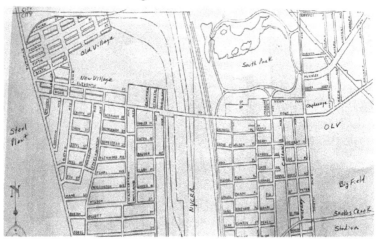

The People of the Neighborhood and Visitors to the Street

It all begins with my cousin, Robert Buchheit. The information on his funeral card reads 1943 to 2009. The date 1943 is important because I cannot remember a time when Robert, or Bobby as he was called, was not around. His mother was my first cousin. We lived six houses apart on Colton Avenue, in Lackawanna, New York. Helen, Bob's mother, and Kay, my mother, were pregnant with each of us at the same time in 1943. How they must have felt with the World War in full tilt, I cannot imagine. Our fathers, John Buchheit, a steelworker and Kelly, my dad, a teacher by day and an airplane factory inspector by night, must have been equally nervous and afraid.

I was born first, on June 28th. Robert would follow on September 29th. Somehow my brain tells me he was there when my memory kicked in.

The term "brunch" was not yet in vogue. We would be at family gatherings almost each Sunday at his grandmother's house, my aunt Liz's. She would expect family members to show up for breakfast or lunch after going to mass. Of course, she had her eight children, either living there or dropping over. Getting to know cousins was easy.

For my cousin Robert Buchheit, (Bobby) and me, the neighborhood was our world, our universe. I was allowed to go by myself to Bob's house, six houses down and across Leo Place, a little used street. We spent much of our days when we were four in his yard, which was much larger than ours, plus they had a vacant lot next door. Fruit trees adorned the yard in which we climbed and played and sometimes ate from. The fragrant lilac bushes became forts and hideaways. Bob's mom was always home and somehow knowing exactly where we were and what we were doing. In my mind she was a hovering angel there to protect us both, as she would do for the rest of her life.

Cousin Robert "Bob" Buchheit

VISITORS TO MY STREET

The street had kids galore, as the post war baby boom had started. There were also older children, like Bob's older brother and sister, Mickey and Betty, and my older brother, Fran, or Frank, as he became known later, all born before the War started. The five of us did not know it back then but our lives would be forever entwined and filled with mutual admiration and respect. Only Robert and my brother Fran have passed on as I write these words. Losing them was like taking the heart out of my childhood.

Bobby Buchheit, Me, Betty Buchheit, brother Fran, and Mickey Buchheit

Almost every house had some children. Many of the fathers were older and thus did not go to war. Most worked for the Bethlehem Steel Company and were crucial to the war effort.

In 1943 there were at least eight pregnant mothers-to-be on Colton and Victory Avenues. It certainly must have been a sight with all those women living within a block of each other and most of them close friends. Beside my mom (me) and my cousin Helen Buchheit (Bobby) there were Mrs. Kitty Butler (Larry), Mrs. Fran Haggerty (Mike), Mrs. Laura Crosta (Patsy), Mrs. Hendra (Fred), Mrs. Baker (Kenny), Mrs. Walsh (Mary Alice,) all from two blocks on Colton. Moving one street over east and west there were Mrs. Gargala (Ruthie), Mrs. Fran Shea (Nan), Mrs. Evelyn Russ (Roger), Mrs. Hartman (Bobby), Mrs. Miller (Bob) and Mrs. Kaney (Helen Marie). All of us would grow up together, go to school together and be lifelong friends except Roger, Fred, and Kenny as they moved away, and we lost contact. Patsy, Bob Buchheit, Bob Miller, Mary Alice Walsh, Fred Hendra, Kenny Baker and Larry Butler have all left us as I write these words. Not sure about Nan Shea or Roger Russ as we lost contact after high school.

Living in a close neighborhood with these 1943 people they became more family than friends. The mothers would treat us all special now that I look back. What wonderful people they all were. I cannot imagine the fear that each of the mothers must have felt bringing a child into a world at war. Luckily, by the time we were all two years old, the war ended, and calm returned to our street. Fathers came home and life took on a peaceful routine with the men working shifts at the Bethlehem Steel Plant and mothers caring for their young in a time of peace and soon to be for some, a little prosperity. One thing that strikes me all these years later is the fact that most, if not all the mothers did not drive. Only one I remembered driving was my cousin Helen. I can remember us kids being in the street and when we saw a woman driving a car we would say, "Get out of the way a woman driver." We must have heard the fathers talk like that. My mom never drove.

I know it is hard for younger generations to imagine just how many young people lived, near each other, on Colton, Victory, Crescent, South Park, Electric and Leo. Just listing "kids" who were within six years of each other in age and living within two blocks of each other may give an idea of unlimited number of potential playmates.

Colton Avenue Residents:

- Bajer, Ray and two brothers
- Baker, Kenny
- Barrett, Audrey, and Robert
- Barrett Tom, Mary Rita, and Eddie
- Buchheit, Betty, Mickey, and Bob
- Butler, Larry
- Callsen, Evie, Paul, and Andrew
- Crosta, Patsy, Clair, and Peggy
- Crosta, John and Leo
- Daley, Tommy, and Maureen
- Daley, Kathleen, Pat, Bernie, Tommy
- Davidson, Bev, and Mary Jane
- DeVaney, Nelson
- Franey, Jennie and Mike
- Galligan, Billy, Pat, and Joey
- Gavin, Billy, and Tommy
- Guarino, Ross Jr., Mary Frances, and Dave
- Haggerty, Mike, Tom, and Sheila

BERNARD T. MCCANN

- Hanley, Dick
- Hendra, Fred, Jim, and Terry
- Janan, Jerry
- Klier, Bobby
- Kogut, Danny, Bernice, and Maryann
- Krupp, Betty Jean
- Lalley, Pat, Peter, and Dennis
- Langan, Mike and Bea
- McCann, Francis, and Bernard
- Merrick, Tom, Mike, Andy, and Mary Ellen
- Noone, Jack, and Linda
- O'Connor, David and his two younger brothers
- O'Leary, Mary Alice
- Osborne, Mike, and Joanne
- Reagan, Eddie
- Rojek, Tom and Frank
- Skipper, Billy, and Gail
- Stieselinger, Brian and Jackie
- Tylock, Frank, Susan, Dorothy, and Judy
- Walsh, Mary Alice

Victory Avenue Residents:

- Bohan, Eileen and Jimmy
- Brooks, Tommy, and Noreen
- Clifford, George, Margaret, Mark, and Timmy
- Fox, Marian, and Margret
- Gallagher, Pat, and Kathleen
- Hartnett, Bob
- Kramer, Sharon
- Kuryak, Jim, John, and Mike
- Lalley, Mimi

- Lillis, Mike, Pat, and Peggy
- Loftus, Patsy
- Malone, Pat
- Meegan, Nancy, Kevin, Steven, Joe, and Theresa
- Miller, Bob, and his twin sisters
- Murphy Judy and Mike
- Shea, Jocko and Jeff
- Shea, Mike, Cathy, and Nan
- Shea, Tom, Danny, and Ann Marie
- Taylor, Bill
- Wenzel, Jim, and John
- Wietchy, Henry
- Young, Sheila, Terry, Ron

Crescent Avenue Residents:

- Baron, Mike, and Billy
- Hartman, Bob, Florence, Mary and Ritchie
- Jenkins, Suzie, and Jimmy
- Russ, Roger

Leo Place Residents:

- Lavell, Helen, and Wilma
- McCann, Billy
- Shultz, Danny & Ron

South Park Residents:

- Albee, Ray
- Curtin, Franky, Billy, and Kelly
- Giblin, Alfred

- Holdren, Billy
- Kaney, Terry and Helen Marie
- McCann, Gary, and Mary Ann
- Rams, Cookie

Electric Avenue Residents:

- Gargala, Ruthie
- O'Neil, Pat "Slick" and Babe
- Shaw, Jim, and John
- Sterlace, Dave
- Tobin, Marty
- Bogacz, Gerald

Maple Grove Residents

- Moran, Cathy, and Maureen

The people listed were mostly within eight years of age with me being in the middle. I was within a couple of years of each of them. I would be considered a playmate of everyone named. The connection could be sports or just neighborhood games. They were schoolmates and close family friends. I may have missed someone and for that I am terribly sorry.

Virtually everyone in the neighborhood was seen into the world by one doctor, Gene Sullivan. Most of the neighbors went to Our Lady of Victory (OLV) Parish, except the Hendra's who were Protestants. Most went to OLV School, with few exceptions as they went to the public school in Lackawanna. Several the parents were teachers, Both Shea families, Guarino, Merrick, Haley, Lalley, Russ, Callsen and our family.

So many of us played sports together, went to school together and were friendly with each other. It was a small community within a small community.

The pace of life was slower, with less information bombarding us each hour. The OLV play yard was a gathering place where we shared softball, basketball, and a myriad of other games that all mentioned above took part in at some time or another.

Uncle's Return After the War

I suppose the first BIG event in my memory, on our street, was the day my uncles, Art, and John (two of mom's brothers) came home from the War. Art was a sergeant in the Army and had spent the war guarding the Panama Canal. (He would stay in the Reserve and eventually retire as Full Bird Colonel.) John was in the Army Air Corp as a Second Lieutenant. His story is closely woven to me. You see I saved his life during the war, . . . maybe. In the fall of 1944, November to be exact, Uncle John had just finished his Officer training to be a Navigator in the United States Army Air Corps (USAAC.) He came to our house where his mom, my grandmother, lived. His training had been in Illinois. Well, I cannot say I remember his coming because I was only one year old. I am told that he wanted to see his newest and soon to be his favorite nephew. I was in a crib and Uncle John stuck his finger in my belly to make me laugh. I took umbrage at this affront to my dignity and promptly stuck my little finger in his eye. That resulted in two weeks at OLV Hospital and a missed transport to Europe. The Battle of the Bulge was just starting and things in Europe were not so good.

John, since he missed his shipment overseas, was re-deployed back to Illinois for renewed training. It was April of 1945 before he completed the course work, and the War in Europe was over. He would be stateside until September of 1945. He was always thankful to me.

Back to the big day. I remember the time very well because my mom and my grandmother went on a cleaning extravaganza the likes of which we had never seen before. Excitement was palpable in the McCann household. Grandma and mom had prayed daily for the boy's safe return and now they were coming home. They were strangers, to me, but I sensed they were important to everybody. These two big guys in crisp uniforms held me and played with me and I soon forgot they were strangers. My mom's other brother, Fran showed up to complete her family reunion. The whole house was aglow with happiness and joy.

My brother Fran and I were extra excited as our uncles brought us gifts. They somehow bought for each of us an Eisenhower jacket. Mine was a pint-sized version of the uniform jacket Ike made famous. In addition, they brought us used ammunition boxes. These were metal and tough. We used them for years to store "stuff."

VISITORS TO MY STREET

*Mom, Uncle Fran, Uncle John, and Uncle Art
(Notice Art is wearing an Eisenhower Jacket)*

The photographer who came to take the pictures of this special day is another story himself, a frequent visitor to many of the homes on our street. His name was Brother John, a member of the, Brothers of the Holy Infancy, which Father Baker founded to help run the OLV Homes of Charity. More on that story later. Somehow this religious Brother would be the chronicler of happy times in our community, from weddings and graduations to celebrating returning soldiers. Our family is blessed with his photos.

I can only imagine the same type of reunions happening to households all over the country with fathers, brothers and sons returning home. Photos were taken and I keep one of them by my desk all these years later. I write these words seventy-two years after the fact.

The story of my veteran uncles is the story of the GI Bill. Both brothers would enroll in the University of Illinois. Apparently Uncle John had been stationed during the war at Chanute Air Force Base located in Champaign County, Illinois, south of and adjacent to Rantoul, Illinois, about 130 miles (210 km) south of Chicago. Its primary mission throughout its existence was Air Force technical training. John was thus familiar with the University of Illinois located at nearby Champaign. Once he enrolled, Uncle Art would shortly follow his older brother.

John would stay on at Illinois after graduating to attend the University of Illinois Law School. They both would meet and marry the loves of their lives my Aunt Laura (Art) and my Aunt Ellen (John). Aunt Ellen made it into her nineties only passing away in 2019.

The summer of 1948 weddings would provide a trip of a lifetime for me as Dad, Mom, Grandma, Fran, and I would travel to Champaign, Illinois for the nuptials. We drove in a four door, dark blue 1948 Kaiser. No radio, so we brought along a very large portable radio that picked up mostly farm related stations. Something I will never forget was stopping in South Bend, IN to visit my Uncle Fran's brother-in-law, Jimmy Madigan. Jimmy was a Holy Cross Brother working at Notre Dame. I knew what Notre Dame was because of dad's

VISITORS TO MY STREET

listening to every Notre Dame Football game, every Saturday afternoon in the fall. The one memory that sticks out was when Jimmy took us down to the stadium field to touch the grass. One of those moments you can never forget. As I got a little older, one of the first books I ever read was *The Life of Knute Rockne*, the legendary coach at Notre Dame. His record at Notre Dame was 105 victories, only twelve loses and five ties. Throw in the three national championships and five undefeated seasons and it is easy to see his contribution to the game. My personal interest in Notre Dame Football would start in the coach Frank Leahy era.

Notre Dame was more than a college or university to OLV parish. Because it was a Catholic University it was symbolic of everything Catholic. The loyalty to Notre Dame, especially in the fall was so strong you could feel it. Saturday afternoon Confessions were heard at OLV Basilica. There were four sets of Confessional with Monsignor Maguire sitting near the railing on the main altar. Each of the four parish priests had their own confessionals so you knew who you were going to for your confession. Monsignor McMahon, the assistant pastor, would expect someone to come along, and in addition to confessing your sins, he would want to know the outcome of the Notre Dame game that Saturday. Confessions started at 4pm so he would not know the final score till after he was in the confessional. No cell phones to tell you, no transistor radios to listen to, so word of mouth was the only alternative.

The other connection to Notre Dame that developed at OLV was Father Baker High School where Holy Cross Fathers would teach. The Holy Cross Fathers also taught at Notre Dame. Their arrival in the early fifties just added to the Notre Dame loyalty amongst the neighborhood people. The second Annual Father Baker's Sport's Night featured then newly appointed football coach at Notre Dame, Terry Brennan. I had his autograph in the program but over the past sixty years I have lost it. Brennan was a player at Notre Dame and a classmate of Father Delonzo, who taught at Father Baker. At the time of writing this I watched a Notre Dame victory on TV in overtime against Clemson, the number one ranked team (Dec. 20, 2020.) All through the game all I could think of was how my dad would have loved that moment.

Father DeLonzo would be the celebrant of the first mass that I ever served. In the early fifties catholic priest had to say daily prayers. The Holy Cross Fathers who taught at Father Baker High School would often be seen walking around the outside of the school saying these prayers. One night we were playing softball at the OLV school yard when someone hit a homerun over the fence. Father DeLonzo was walking past, his head in his prayer book. Without blinking an eye, he dropped his book and caught that home run. He threw the ball back over the fence, picked up his book and continued walking as if nothing had happened. Little did I know then that he had been a football lineman for Notre Dame.

Sorry for the diversion, we were going to weddings. The weddings took place a week apart. It seemed we were there for a long time. I have visual images of the wedding and of meeting the Decker's (Laura) and the O'Donnell's (Ellen).

The two uncles would eventually settle in Lackawanna. John would become the Secretary of the Lackawanna Chamber of Commerce and had a management position at the Plant before moving to Akron, Ohio as the Treasurer of B. F. Goodrich Corporation. Art would work his way up to a management position at the plant. He would also continue his military career serving in the Army Reserve, rising to the rank of Full Colonel in the 277th Quartermaster Corp. He would at one point be the company commander for my cousin Mickey Buchheit when they were both in the Reserves.

On the way home we added Art and Laura to the Kaiser. I do remember spending time on the floor of the back seat. Mostly, I remember passing field after field of corn growing so high it was like we were driving in a tunnel.

One soldier who did not return was Sgt. James H. Hanley 32375419, US Army, who lived directly across the street at 69 Colton. His story was related to me years later by his sister Mary Hanley, who would have a profound impact on my life. Jim was assigned to the Burma Theater in WW II. He was killed in Burma. Mary, who worked at City Hall, heard someone talking about another death of a Lackawanna man. Death notices to families at that time came through City or Town governments. She then heard the name Hanley mentioned. She optimistically thought it was another Hanley from our neighborhood whose death was announced the previous week. She went home not too concerned. When she arrived home, her mother, Brigid was crying, and Mary realized how wrong she had been. This was in 1945 when I was two years old. Jim would be buried in a military cemetery in Burma. After the war, his body was sent to a military cemetery in Hawaii. Around 1948 he was again reinterred and brought back to Lackawanna for a funeral mass and burial in Holy Cross Cemetery. I would attend that funeral. Poor Mrs. Hanley would have to relive those horrible feelings of loss all over again. At least, she had her son home now, not buried in a distant place. Again, this event was replaying itself all over America. Bodies were returned, others stayed in those far-away places. That is one of the reasons so many Americans visit the American cemeteries in France and Germany.

In 2009, I had occasion to be visiting a former exchange

student of mine in Germany, Lisa Hodey. Lisa and her dad took me to see interesting sites from a former Roman settlement that had been recreated as a museum to ancient monasteries. The most interesting place they took me was a War Cemetery almost exclusively of British Airmen. There were also Americans buried there. The German Government maintains this and other "foreign" cemeteries. Each grave site had a red rosebush in front of it. As you walk along the rows of headstones you can read the dates of death. It was clear that five or six in a row would all have the same date of death, indicating that their plane was shot down and they all died together. The dates of birth were even more telling as the enlistees were all 18 or 19 years of age while the officers were no more than 22 or 23. Lisa and I were both in tears after a few minutes of walking down the rows of monuments to the sacrifice of these brave young men. So many lives snuffed out about the time that I was born. While I was in my first two years on that safe and sacred ground of Colton Avenue, these men, and thousands more were having their lives destroyed, just like Jim Hanley.

Lisa and her dad also took me to a German War Cemetery. The buried men, or more rightly I should call them boys, as their ages were anywhere from, seventeen to eighteen, and most died in 1944 and 1945.

Brigid Hanley

The Hanley family would be a significant influence in my life for decades to come. Mr. and Mrs. Hanley were immigrants from Ireland and bought their home on Colton from

Father Baker. One of Father Baker's projects was to provide decent housing for the Catholic families working at the steel mills. More on that later. Mr. Hanley had a brogue so thick it was awfully hard to understand him. In later years I would tell people that I did not have to kiss the Blarney Stone because Mrs. Hanley had kissed it and then kissed me. I have been told my gift of gab is something very real. Thank you, Mrs. Hanley. She was the kindly grandmother for the whole street and the one person you could count on having a good word for you no matter the time or place.

There were six boys and one girl, James, Patrick, John, Vincent, Mickey, Charles, and Mary. James was the one who died in WWII. They were all bachelors who lived at home their whole lives except Mickey who married and moved away. Mary never married and would live in the house well into her eighties, her siblings having all predeceased her.

Mickey was a bigger than life figure for my cousin Bob and me. Mick was a deputy sheriff for Erie County, who was on motorcycle patrol. He would often stop at his mother's house, in uniform and with his motorcycle. He would often let us sit on the motorcycle and pretend we were riding. He sometimes had passes to the Erie County Fair each August in Hamburg. He generously would give Robert and me tickets in the hopes our parents would take us. After Mick married and left Colton, he would then become one of our cherished visitors. Sadly, shortly after he was married, he passed away. He left a large void on the street and in the Colton community and in his mother's heart.

Chuck Hanley was a bricklayer. At one point, the Hanley's added a garage in their back yard. Chuck laid all the bricks. He would let me be a sort of "gopher," mostly getting lemonade from his mother to help cool him off. He had friends helping sometimes. I guess they were his union buddies. The building of the garage changed our playing area forever. More about our neighborhood-wide games later.

Chuck had somehow also learned to cut hair. One day Father Baker asked him to cut his hair. Chuck would, of course, say yes. While cutting the possible future saint's hair, Chuck collected a fair amount of it and brought it home. He kept it for years. At one point, a friend of his was gravely ill. His sister Mary offered to let the family of the sick friend take the hair. The man recovered, but the sick man's family never returned the hair.

Return to Plattsburgh for Mom

While the trip to Illinois was long and difficult, we would take a much more enjoyable trip to mom's alma mater, Plattsburgh State Normal, now SUNY Plattsburgh a year later. The trip began by way of Canada up to Toronto. All I remember about Toronto was that they were building a subway system, so the place was all torn up, with piles of dirt everywhere.

Next stop was in Ottawa, Canada's capital. I distinctly remember the Natural History Museum. The huge dinosaurs would leave an impression on a young boy. Years later, while on a business trip to Ottawa, I made a point to go to that same museum and it looked exactly as my little boy memory pictured it.

From Ottawa we went to Montreal, but I am not sure if we stayed there, but we drove through it. Plattsburgh, NY was only an hour or so from Montreal.

Mom must have been disoriented because, the one classroom building she had attended burned to the ground her last year at State Normal. By 1949 there were new buildings for her to see.

I do remember going swimming in Lake Champlain. My little brain was making comparisons with the same activity in Lake Erie. Erie had nice sandy beaches and the bottom was all sand. Champlain was not clear, and no sand on the beaches or bottom. It did not leave a very favorable impression with me. While not a good swimming lake, it certainly is beautiful with the Adirondacks to the west and Green Mountains to the east. Living near Lake Champlain for much of my adult life has made me appreciate its grandeur and majesty.

Mom would have enjoyed the fact that I became an adjunct professor at SUNY Plattsburgh where I would teach a course in Education Law for two summers. In addition, I would teach a Plattsburgh College course to high school students at North Warren High School and visiting the campus for three days each year.

The next stops were something I will never forget, Crown Point and Fort Ticonderoga. Both places were ingrained in my memory because of the scale of both and I guess my innate sense of history at an early age. As I write this, it was just yesterday that I drove past Crown Point, which is only an hour from my Adirondack home. We often visit the State Park at Crown Point. In winter it is a cold and lonely place. The ruins are bare and empty, yet they seem to echo voices from the past. Crown Point is one of my favorite places because I shared it with Mom, Dad and Fran.

Fort Ti, as it is called around here, was only open a year or so in 1949. In 1777, the British, destroyed the fort, as they retreated north after the defeat at Saratoga. The Mars Candy people were instrumental in bringing the Fort back to its revolutionary self. I remember sitting on the canons and being amazed by the scope of the place.

Fran and I fighting off the British at Fort Ti in 1949

One other instance I recall from that visit to the fort was Fran trying to convince me that the larger than life, statues of colonial soldiers were real people. He did scare me as they were very menacing to a little kid.

When my grandson Adam was three years old, I took him to Fort Ti and he loved it as much as I did when I was little.

The odyssey continued to Lake George, where I remember swimming in that very cold lake. Little did I know that Lake George would become my home 30 years later. The Plattsburgh trip would be a foreshadowing of my later life. We traveled on to Albany where mom had finished her BA degree and she wanted to show us where she attended. All I remember was that we went to Sunday mass at a large cathedral. I took ill during the service, so mom took me outside and walked up and down the street. Just like Plattsburgh and Lake George I would return to Albany to attend Albany Law School in 1965. Mom would have liked the idea that I would also eventually receive my master's degree in Education from SUNY Albany.

The trip would continue across New York State in pre-Thruway time. We would take Routes 5 or 20 across the state to Buffalo and home. There is so much about that trip that influenced the rest of my life. Thanks to mom and dad for instilling in me a love of travel that has taken me all over the United States and the world.

In Car Games

What did little kids do while traveling long distance in the car? There were no videos sets, no radio and reading made us car sick. Therefore, games had to be devised to keep us from asking, "Are we there yet?" One of the simplest was merely counting the telephone poles. That one lost its luster real fast. License plate games kept you attuned to out of state cars. I "SPY" was a favorite and we still play that with our grandchildren. When all else failed you simply took a nap.

In the Greater World

The year was 1948 and the world was a peaceful place, at least in Champaign, Illinois. The world was actually in turmoil. The Chinese Revolution and the India Partition wars were creating chaos. The summer Olympics were happening in London. Two of my favorite books were published that year, Norman Mailer's *The Naked and the Dead* and *The Plague* by Albert Camus. Orville Wright would pass away, and Truman's improbable election would occur that November and Joseph McCarthy, was terrorizing Hollywood Producers.

Front Porches

Porches of Colton Avenue were a thing of pride and comfort. In the years before air-conditioning people routinely spent the hot months on their porches. Once Memorial Day was over, brooms would get to work sweeping away the winter grime. Most houses had nice shades to block the afternoon sun or to just give a greater sense of privacy. Our porch was covered with carpets that we rolled up each evening in case of rain. The carpets gave a feeling of being in a real room. There was a wonderful glider where I spent hours napping or reading. Its gentle swaying back and forth was conducive to a nice nap. Maybe that is where I engendered my propensity for the proverbial catnap.

I recently found letters my mom wrote while on the front porch. She and dad would sit out on the porch after supper, just like every other neighbor. It would be the second week of July 1951. My brother Fran was away at a Boy Scout Camp, near Arcade NY, called Camp Ti-Wa-Ya-Ee. Mom would write five letters to him making sure he knew she was worried about him. I decided to print these letters verbatim as they reflect a simpler time when families were close knit.

July 15, 1951, Sunday Evening
Dear Francis,

> *I suppose by now you are all settled and know where you are going to sleep. I do hope you are satisfied with whatever arrangements are. Try to be pleased dear – there are so many things worse that could happen to you that I hate to see you unhappy about something like that.*
>
> *John Buchheit took Betty Ann, Bobby, and Bernard out to Hamburg on the Lake this afternoon. Bernard is a little uncomfortable from sunburn as a result. He is laying on the cot at the present. Dad, Grandma and I sat on the porch I wrote a few letters and then we took the document about the relic back to Nash's. We stayed there about an hour Betty's children are darling. We had some birch beer and cookies.*
> *They wanted us to stay for supper.*

Jackie (my cousin Johnny McDonnell) dropped in for a few minutes. Daddy made us some bacon, lettuce, and tomato sandwiches _ we have the dishes done and are back sitting on the porch

Fran, I wish you would try and write a little note to Sister M. Concepta

And thank her for the stamps. She will be interested in anything you have to say. I'll put her address on the front of this paper.

Don't forget to say some extra prayers for me Tuesday, that's the day I'll be in the hospital. Be a good boy and take care of Mickey (Buchheit cousin) and Tommy (Shea, neighbor). Tommy's mother called me up tonight.

Take care of yourself _ with all my love.
Mother

Monday Night (7/16/51)
Dear Fran,

This was a nice day here (Meaning Sunday) hope it was nice at camp.

Dad and I got up and went to 7 O'clock to receive Holy Communion. We came home – ate breakfast and left (Grandma, Bernard, Dad, and I) for the Carmelite Convent where *we attended the Pontifical Mass said by Bishop O'Hara with nine priest and six altar boys serving him. It was the 700th anniversary of Our Lady of Mount Carmel giving the scapular to Saint Simon Stock. After Mass, the Bishop came down the aisle and blessed everyone. When he came back, we were up at the alter railing lighting candles and he passed us – blessing us again. We were sorry you were not along.*

Bernard got a bad burn yesterday. The two days in a row were more than his skin could take. He spent all afternoon playing with his blocks in the house.

We are all sitting on the porch listening to the radio. Art and Laura are here.

It is very peaceful around here – I wonder why?

Imagine those bills Dad gave you are rubber, stretch them out to last the week.

With much love,
Dad, Bernard and Mom & Grandma, Art, and Laura

Monday Night (7/16/51) second letter
Dear Francis,

Well, how are you doing? It seems so funny

without you. I slept in your bed last night. Bernard didn't want to be alone the first night.

We had rain on and off all day. I didn't wash, so we went and bought the paint and daddy started painting. He did the front hall.

Uncle Art (mom's brother) came by last night. Aunt Laura went back to Champlain with her mother and father.

Tuesday 7/17/51 (Continued on same paper) I didn't have quite enough to say so I decided not to mail it until today. It has rained off and on again today. Do hope the weather is better out your way.

Daddy painted all day. We are really all torn up downstairs.

Be a good boy and take care of yourself.

With lots of love,
Daddy, Bernard, Grandma and Mother

PS
Didn't know I had this space left? Bernard has formed a club The "Crab Apple Club" they call themselves. Dues are a penny. They have been collecting member s all afternoon. Daddy and I had to join.

Well dear you notice my pen went dry. (Faded writing)
Love Mom

Thursday Afternoon, 7/19/51
Dear Fran,

Received your card yesterday. I went into the hospital at 8:15 Tuesday morning and was there until 5 PM. They gave me only a local anesthetic, so I was conscious of everything they were doing to my throat. They put me to bed before and after. I had to go to bed as soon as I got home and stayed there until today. I can't eat much – just a liquid diet mostly milk, so I have been weak. However, I feel much better tonight.

Everyone has been lovely to me. – all the cards, letters, etc. that I am receiving and prayers it seems as if everyone I know is praying and offering up novenas for me.
Fran and Ross (Guarino) *went down to Leroy yesterday and brought back a huge bouquet of all kinds of flowers – two quarts of raspberries and three head of lettuce out of Ross's Dad's Garden.*

Laura has been here helping Grandma all day.

Cathy Kane (my cousin) *was in from Lockport today. Take care of yourself – hope you didn't have that bad thunderstorm we had last night.*

With love from us all,
Mom, Dad, Bernard & Grandma

BERNARD T. MCCANN

Thursday Night, 7/19/51
Dear Francis,

Mary Galligan (Neighbor, mother of Joey who was with Fran) called me up last night when she came back from camp. I'm sorry you didn't receive my letter, but I imagine you did today

We received your letter and card and are glad you are enjoying yourself. Do be careful and don't get hurt.

We had a little excitement on the street today. They had a fire in Krupp's basement. It seems the refrigerator motor burned out. We were sitting on the porch when Al Haggerty ran up and pulled the alarm box. (There were fire alarm boxes placed strategically in each neighborhood)
We are planning on coming out Saturday afternoon. So, take care of yourself.

With Love from all of us,
Mother

PS I'm enclosing a dollar.

My mom had a large tumor on her neck. It was the size of a baseball. The doctors did not get all the cancer out of my mom. She would die less than a year later. These are the only letters of hers that have survived. They tell the story of a tight knit community of friends and relations who cared deeply about each other. It was a time of radio, slow communications, and letter writing. It was a time of simple joy of sitting on one's front porch talking, listening to the portable radio, and greeting friends who stopped by to chat. There was a connectivity to society that is almost gone today. I heard my daughter Brigid tell how during the Covid-19 pandemic her apartment complex neighbors would distance socially and enjoy each other's company. That is the way things were every night in summer on Colton Avenue in Lackawanna in the forties and fifties.

Nearly every family had a glider or a combination of wooden rockers and/or metal chairs. The Hanley's porch was the only one on the street that was screened in. That alone made it an especially nice place to congregate. My grandma Moran would often walk across the street to visit with Mrs. Hanley and Mary, her daughter. Her brothers were also present. They all loved just sitting there and talking and watching the sidewalk traffic which often brought more people to the porch. In the late forties there was no television and even the radio shows in the summer would be repeats. So outside you would go to meet other people. It was as if the street emptied its houses and put people in touch with one another through their porches. Maybe that explains how well all the neighbors got along. The people of Colton were always; helping one another, watching out for older and younger residents and generally being friendly and nice. I cannot think of one person on the street who was not nice. I would be invited to stay for lunch, which I often did, either at Butler's with my friend Larry or Haggerty's with Mike and Tom or my cousin Bob's or Guarino's right next door.

Mentioning Larry Butler, we were both born in the same hospital two weeks apart. Our mothers had spent their pregnancies together. That bond would continue through our high school years. Larry would pass away tragically in a choking accident shortly after having his first and only child. I was away in the Army when that happened and was not able to return home for the funeral. Not being able to say good-bye has bothered me all these years. Larry's mom would pass shortly after his death.

Mystery Solved

For most of my life I wondered about three houses on our street. They were all fancy cement block houses while all the other houses were wood frame or brick. The houses, in question, were three in a row below Berry Street on Colton. They all had members of the Crosta Family living in them. My dear friend Peggy Crosta Burke recently sent me a part of a book called *History of the Niagara Frontier,* which detailed the achievements of her grandfather, John H. Crosta. As a small boy, I remember Mr. Crosta and his wife living in the middle of the three houses. He was always a very congenial older gentleman. The article opened my eyes to a real community hero.

Mr. Crosta was born in Philadelphia in 1873. That would put him at 73 years of age when my memory of him kicked in. His father, according to the article, was a renowned general contractor. John would leave school to apprentice with his dad. After a time, he would go on his own as a general contractor. One of his achievements was that he oversaw building the famous Atlantic City Boardwalk.

Eventually, in 1900, he would find himself in the hamlet of Limestone Hill, part of West Seneca, NY and now

Lackawanna. He started a general contracting and cement block business. Hence, the three houses he would build for his family were all cement blocks. Mystery solved. Thank you, Peggy.

But Mr. Crosta did so much more for his local community. In 1910, he worked hard to turn his new hometown into the City of Lackawanna. He was active in the Moose, the Elks, the selling of War Bonds during World War Two, active in local politics, once running unsuccessfully for Mayor, served on the Board of a local Bank, and served on the Lackawanna School Board for fourteen years. In addition, he bought the local Ford Motor dealership and ran that successful business.

In short, he was a model citizen who added to the betterment of Lackawanna. All his grandchildren would be my friends and playmates.

Milk Right to Your Home

Back home and life continued. I am sorry I got sidetracked again. The street visitors would be a constant amusement for Bob and me. Take Jim the milkman from Sterling Amherst. He was so nice. His arrival on the street would find Bob and me sitting on the side steps at Bob's house. The two of us would spends endless hours on those steps just talking and watching the street scene until we were both out of high school. Sometimes his dad, John Buchheit, would join us. It was always an education listening to John. He talked to us as if we were adults and would explain many of life's mysteries.

Jim, the milkman would arrive around ten in the morning. He serviced the Barrett house across the street and then

Buchheit's. One cool thing about Bob's house was that it had a special small door near the back entrance where the milkman could leave the delivery and pick up the empties. On the inside of the house, you could access this area and get your milk without going outside. Bob and I would leave messages in there sometimes.

After his deliveries near Bob's, he would let us get in his truck to get a piece of ice. Ice cubes were the only refrigerant in the truck. His next stop was my house, and he would let us ride up the street with him. Jim would put the milk bottles inside our side doorway and take the returns. One of my jobs was to put the clean return bottles there and to put away the new bottles. That milk was so good. The cream was still on the top when you took off the little cardboard cover. Once in a great while mom would order Chocolate milk and what a treat that would be for us. Today, Jim would be crucified for doing such a thing but back then it was an adventure for us and not frowned upon. Looking back, I am sure he was a returning war veteran. He always made two, four-year old kids very happy.

Bakery Deliveries

Friday would see any number of visitors to Colton. Our favorite was Gerry the Baker man from Hall's Bakery. This was how people got their bread products. We did not get regular deliveries from Jerry but occasionally mom would order Raisin Bread from him. He would not leave the products outside. Every house allowed him to go inside and put the bread in a breadbox. Unthinkable today but then common trust was a real thing. Gerry had a great sense humor. He was always kidding us children. He always had a smile on his face and a good word to all his customers. As a Cub Scout we toured the Hall's Bakery in Buffalo. I spent the entire tour looking for Jerry. But, of course, he was out making deliveries.

Fresh Eggs

The next Friday visitor was Don the Egg Man. He arrived late in the afternoon and would leave a dozen or two of eggs that came freshly laid from his farm somewhere to the south of Lackawanna. He was quiet but very nice with a quick smile. Since he came later in the day my mom would be home from school and engaged him in conversation.

The Insurance Man

The last Friday visitor was Mr. Kelly the Insurance man. He would park his car somewhere on the street and then start walking from house to house. He was collecting premiums that people would pay once a week for life insurance. He had a large book that held receipts. I can see him sitting down at my dad's desk handing dad such a receipt for that week's payment. I do not know how much but the payment was, but it was always in coin, so it had to be less than a dollar. He would always chat a while and then off to the next house.

Only after my dad passed did I learn that the policies were for only two thousand dollars.

Bees

An often summertime visitor was the Bumble Bee. It had to be in the later forties on a sunny summer day. I was playing in the back yard and suddenly, I had this horrible sting, as a bee got me on the arm. Mom rushed out when she heard my cry. She went into first aid mode at once. She had Fran get dirt and she began rubbing the dirt on the affected area. The pain decreased and I calmed down. She held me for a long time then cleaned the dirt off and put on a bandage. I was all better. I never forgot the dirt.

Neighborhood Mailman

Someone who came six days a week was Ed Breen. Mr. Breen was the mailman. He also lived in the neighborhood, so we knew him as a neighbor and as a visitor. He would often let me walk along with him as he went up the street. Cannot remember what we talked about, but he always had time for a little kid's questions. What people today would find astonishing is he came both in the morning and in the afternoon on weekdays and once in the morning on Saturdays. He was part of the ebb and flow of the days on Colton. I am sure people kept track of time by his deliveries. Two weeks out of every year Mr. Breen would not be on his route. It was typical for American workers, in 1948, to get a two-week vacation. Fran and I were lucky as mom and dad being schoolteachers had the summers off.

The Basilica and Father Baker

People on the street and in the neighborhood did not need Mr. Breen to figure out the time. We lived in the shadow of one of the largest churches in the United States, Our Lady of Victory Basilica. On the quarter hour and on the half hour and on every hour the church bells would sound. On the hour they would ring the same number as the hour. On the half hour it played a little melody. The quarter hour was just a few rings. At six in the evening, it played the Angelus. The bells were a comforting sound that blanketed the area with the protective vigilance of the Basilica and Father Baker.

I suppose this is as good a place as any to talk about one of the strongest influences on my life. He was a man I never met, yet I felt as if I knew him all my life. That man was the Reverend Monsignor Nelson Baker. He and the Basilica would have a large influence on the rest of my life and that of many others. As I got older and could be farther from home on summer nights the nine o'clock bells would start to ring, and I would better be home by the ninth toll as my curfew was nine o'clock.

I will not try to tell his entire story as that would take volumes and others have already done so. Father Baker, as he was affectionately called, was the pastor of the Basilica and the Administrator of the OLV Homes of Charity. At the intersection of Ridge Road and South Park Avenue (two blocks away from Colton) was found the Basilica and a Boys Orphanage, a very large building, called the Protectory, a Home for unwed mothers, an infant home, a convent, a school, and a hospital. These and more enterprises such as the Working Boys Home in Buffalo and a farm found about a mile away made up the Homes of Charity. Up until the end of the Great Depression over a thousand boys lived in the Protectory Building where they lived and learned trades such as, barbering, shoemaking, electronics, carpentry, bricklaying and more. The buildings (both four stories and "L" shaped) were mostly empty by the time 1948 came along. There was still a gymnasium where we could learn about boxing and wrestling. My brother Fran would sometimes take me there. One of the buildings would be repurposed in the fifties, into a Catholic Boys High School named for Father Baker. It would eventually evolve into a co-institutional high school called Baker-Victory. I would spend four happy years in that building.

Father Baker died at age 94 on July 29, 1936, seven years before I was born. Every year on that date there is a special celebration at the basilica to honor Father Baker. The city would proclaim that day, Father Baker's Day. His funeral mass was repeated, and huge crowds would attend. After mass there would be a procession from the church to his gravesite at nearby Holy Cross Cemetery. Our family took part in the mass and procession each year. My parents knew him personally. He never turned anyone away. He raised money to keep everything afloat and to pay for the Basilica which was debt free on the day of its consecration. His story was always being retold or new anecdotes would be added so that he seemed alive to me. His holiness and goodness were always keys to the stories. My mom would relate that she would stop at the basilica each day after school. Invariably she would meet him saying the Stations of the Cross. Father Baker is now a candidate for sainthood. His body has been placed inside the basilica in front of a side altar. I only hope I live long enough to go to Rome to be at his canonization. He may not have been a physical visitor to the street, but his presence was very much omnipresent, at least on the hour and half hour and quarter hour of every day.

There are two biographies of Father Baker; *Father of the Fatherless: The Authorized Biography of Father Nelson Baker* – May 2, 2011 by Richard Gribble CSC, and *Father Baker,* by Floyd Anderson | Jan 1, 1960. Anderson expanded his first work with, *Apostle of Charity: The Father Nelson Henry Baker Story,* by Floyd Anderson and Illustrated with Photographs | Jan 1, 2002

For those unfamiliar with the OLV Basilica, it is one of the most beautiful churches in the United States, if not the world. It is made of white marble on the outside and multi-color marble on the inside. The artwork and stain glass windows are what you expect from European Cathedrals. Father Baker while a seminarian went on a European tour that exposed him to the great churches of Europe. When planning his church, he used elements from those beautiful churches. The Stations of the Cross lining the side aisles are all life size and carved out of a single marble stone.

The Thirteenth Station of the Cross

The main altar is like the main altars of both St. Peter's in Rome and Notre Dame in Paris, at least, before the tragic fire in 2019. Whenever I am asked about the Basilica, I remind people that God is everywhere, but He lives at Our Lady of Victory Basilica.

Sounds of the Plant

About sounds covering the neighborhood, I neglected to explain that it was very noisy twenty-four seven. It is just that the people of Lackawanna became immune to the sounds, so I do not think in terms of it being noisy. The sounds emanated from the largest steel mill in the United States, the Bethlehem Steel Corporation plant no more than a mile away from our house. Twenty-five thousand men were employed at this one plant that operated all day, every day. The smokestacks constantly belched out tons of smoke and particles. In the summer we had to dust the inside of the house every day. The Open Hearth would drain the slag (impurities) into Lake Erie every so often causing a very loud explosion followed by the sky turning deep red. We had gorgeous artificial sunsets all night long.

Constant Train Traffic

Another ubiquitous sound was that of train traffic. Only three blocks away was the main line of the New York Central

RR. There were at least ten tracks, and a train was moving through town all the time. A flash back to my dad took place on one of these tracks. When dad was about ten, he was crossing the tracks when he was run over by a train. The train wheel ran over his toe. He had the scar forever. His friends carried him home. Unfortunately, that was all the story I got.

Infants Out for a Walk

One scene from our street that will always stay with me was the little parade that walked by almost every day. There would be a line of very young children, maybe two or three years old, walking up or down the street with a rope line attached to each to make sure they were safe. These were children from the Father Baker's Infant Home. There would usually be about ten to fifteen kids in the line with two women escorting them. The women were always quite pregnant, as they were given a place to live until their babies were due. More times than not, their baby would stay at the Infant Home until adopted. Father Baker never allowed these young women to be ashamed of their status. His compassion was ahead of its time for agencies such as the Infant Home.

"Rags – Ragideh"

Again, speaking of noise there was a visitor to the street who would herald his arrival with a call of "Rags, any Rags today." The Ragman came once a month or so but never in winter. He had a cart with single horsepower. For us kids he was a heroic figure, a Don Quixote, with his knightly steed, Rocinante. Just like Rocinante, the horse was quite run-down and the man, I never knew a name except Ragman, was much disheveled like the product he was looking for. Women in the neighborhood could earn a few pennies by selling him old clothes or rags or old newspapers. He would then resell them to a dealer who would recycle or sell to a recycler. His cry "Rags - Ragideh" would be repeated by all of us little kids. He would park his cart just below our house as that put him in the middle of the block under a large shade tree. By the early fifties he just stopped showing up. He could have died, or the economics of the business was no longer practical.

In 1972 my family traveled to Panama where we stayed with my then sister-in-law Mary Heim. Her husband George was a Naval Commander. On a side trip to Costa Rica, we met a friend of Mary's named Jim Stanley. He was retired US Navy, married to a Costa Rican, and lived in San Juan. Jim ran a factory that made native blankets. He would import rags from all over the world except the United States. The material was carded and then pressed into a blanket form. These he would sell throughout Latin America for the equivalent of one US dollar. The factory had ten or so employees. It was obvious to us that the employees loved Jim. We could see he treated them with respect. I tell this only because I wonder if our Ragman sold his rags to a similar outfit.

Get Your Fresh Vegetables

Another summer and fall visitor to the street was the Vegetable Man. He too would arrive with a horse drawn wagon. The vegetables would hang precipitously off the sides of the wagon. They were all fresh and I assume came from his farm somewhere close by. The mothers would come out to check what he had that week. Usually, late afternoon was his timetable.

Never knew his name or where he came from. He just added color and good taste to the neighborhood. He also gave the women a chance to meet and talk right there on the street. During daytime, the women rarely got out of the house. With cleaning, washing/ironing and meal preparation a women's day was easily filled. That reminds me of the famous line, "A man can work from sun to sun, but a woman's work is never done."

Transportation

Not that all families had cars in 1948. Public transportation came from busses going east west on Ridge Road (Buffalo Transit Company) and the trolley car going north on South Park, at the end of the Buffalo City Park known as South Park. By July of 1950, the era of the Streetcar was over. The Niagara Frontier Transit (NFT) bus company would take over the South Park to Triangle to downtown route. I would ride that bus route right up to 1967 when I was clerking for Offerman, Fallon and Mahoney, a law firm in the Statler Hotel downtown.

The Streetcar died because of lack of flexibility to extend into the suburbs and to change routes easily. People wanted cars in the post war era, and they were determined to use them. On my last trip to Buffalo, I read about political interest in bringing back the Trolley Cars. Interesting but not very practical.

Get Your Knives Sharpened

Back to the visitors, and the Knife Sharpening man. He would appear in the spring and summer. One day you would see him carrying his round sharpening stone attached to legs that would open when he set up shop outside someone's house. Sharp knives were important for homemakers who cooked most meals from scratch. They had to do cutting and dicing. He always did a brisk business. Bob and I would love to watch him at work with sparks flying and a grinding noise filling the air. He would disappear sometime in the early fifties.

Fuller Brush Man

A visitor to every neighborhood in the country was the Fuller Brush Man. It seemed there was a different one each year. I do not recall how often he came but it must have been at least three of four times a year. My grandmother oversaw buying the brushes. We never got many brushes, but I recall the one brush used in the bathtub for scrubbing my feet which were always dirty from playing outside. It hurt, especially when grandma would use it on me. You do not forget those type of things easily.

Workers at the Plant

They were not visitors to the street but their movements up and down the street were as regular as rain. These were the men who lived on the street and worked at Bethlehem Steel. The plant operated on three shifts 11PM to 7 AM, 7 AM to 3PM and 3PM to 11PM. The men's shifts were rotated one to the other, so you went from nights to mornings to afternoons and then back to nights. I remember it was two weeks on each shift. It was easy to tell if they were going or coming from work. The returning men were black in the face and their clothes were filthy. On the street you had to be careful not to make too much noise near a house where the father was working the night shift as they were asleep during the day. Often kids would forget or just not know that someone was sleeping, and we would hear it from the mother or worse yet from the offended father. It was just another part of the ebb and flow of life on Colton and other streets in Lackawanna or for that matter in any mill town in the United States where shift work was the rule.

Ice

Another visitor to the street, at least for a little while, was the iceman. He would bring blocks of ice to the few people who still had "iceboxes." There were few customers, and I cannot remember where he stopped. By the late forties or early fifties if you wanted blocks of ice you could go across the railroad tracks where there was a block ice machine was found. Put a coin in and a big block of ice came out. We only got them for when we had picnics at Chestnut Ridge. The blocks kept the beer and soda nice and cold.

Garbage

One of the more mundane visitors came every week. I seem to remember the men coming from the truck, right to your yard to carry the garbage cans out to the truck. Very different from when on designated days garbage cans are left on the street facing a certain way so that the truck driver can drop a lift to pick up the can and dump its contents into the truck. There was another group who also came once a week in the cold months. They were the Ash Collectors. This we had to put outside for them. In the forties and early fifties just about everyone heated their homes with coal. The ashes had to go somewhere. I really do not know where they took it.

Coal

Our coal furnace was also a major attraction for a little boy. It was a monster, taking up a good part of the basement with its large round ductwork and a big furnace proper. The coal was stored in a bin, right under a window. That window would allow the next visitor, the coal delivery man to back into our driveway and position the side coal chute right by the window. Up went the truck bed and down went the coal with all the dust and dirt it could possibly provide.

At Bob's house it was even more fun to watch. Their house had a special metal opening just for coal deliveries. The truck would back onto the sidewalk and put the long shoot into the opening, raise the truck bed and down came the coal. Only took minutes for the whole task but we were fascinated all the same.

I knew I was getting older when dad allowed me a chore of taking ash out of the furnace bottom. And then I really knew I was getting bigger when he allowed me to add coal to the furnace. Not sure parents would allow that today, but I know how proud I was that he let me do it.

Today I have returned to the coal business. My wife Kathy and I added a family room to our house, where a woodshed once existed. We decided we would use a coal stove which works marvelously. In the cold weather I empty the ash every morning. Once a week I take the ash to our local town transfer station and leave the ash in the debris containers. Makes me think of our Colton house every time I work with the ash.

The were no blowers on the furnace. The heat just rose naturally. I remember sitting by a register on evenings when, as a family, would listen to the radio. There was a big console radio in the living room. In the late forties RADIO was still king.

Television

The first TV on our street went to the Stieselinger family when they won a radio DJ contest, which later in life I thought was ironic, a radio program giving away a television. It had an eight-inch screen. Everyone on the street was jealous though they just did not know why. Nobody had even seen a TV. The Stieselinger family had two boys, Jackie, and Brian. The youngest Brian would sometimes play with Robert and me. The family would move away to Orchard Park in the early fifties. During high school I read the sports pages avidly. I would see Brian's name in the basketball box scores for Orchard Park High School. It turned out we would both go to Niagara University. He was one year ahead of me, but we renewed that childhood friendship right away. Unfortunately, he would pass away at an all too young age.

In 1951 the McCann's got a television. Not just any TV, but a Crosley Console that came with an AM and FM Radio and a 33, 45, and 78 speed record player. The screen was ten inches. It sat in the living room where we would gather as soon as 4:30 PM when the Test Pattern would appear to begin the day of TV programming. The day would end around eleven-thirty with the playing of the National Anthem. The only stations were CBS, ABC and NBC. A little antenna sat on the top of the TV. Sometimes I would be asked to stand with it in my hand and then move around the room to find the best reception. I wonder what sort of wave lengths have run through my body because of that.

The first show of the day was Hoody Doody and Buffalo Bob along with twenty-six more characters such as, Dilly Dally, Claribel, (who would go on to become Captain Kangaroo) and so many more. Of course, there was the Peanut Gallery where kids were the audience and would hoot and holler from the bleachers, at the antics of the cast. Claribel was always running after someone spaying them with his seltzer bottle and sometimes, he would hit Buffalo Bob. That was never good. I loved every minute of the show.

Sometime in the afternoon the Kate Smith Show would come on. Grandma always wanted to watch Kate. Even a little boy could appreciate such a fine voice. I still get chills when I hear a recording of her singing, "God Bless America."

Sports was mostly local with exciting Curling from Toronto, Bowling from Buffalo and Boxing every Wednesday night and Friday night. Dad loved to watch Boxing as he did quite a bit of boxing in his youth.

My first introduction to drama was on Friday nights. Dad seemed to be always teaching night school so gramma and I would watch the CBS show, "I Remember Mama," starring Peggy Wood. It was about a Norwegian immigrant family and their daily life. It gave us their experiences in financial troubles, medical woes, and flights of happiness. It was a story about life that ran from July 1, 1949, to March 17, 1957, all through my elementary school years and would have a profound effect on how I saw things that were happening to my family.

Radio

What did we listen to on the radio? Adventures of all sorts would come into our house every evening, from the Shadow to Crime Busters. Bing Crosby had a show and Bob Hope was always around for a laugh. Burns and Allen, Ozzie and Harriet, The Lone Ranger, Amos, and Andy would all make the transition from radio to TV. There was a nightly radio line up of shows too many to list them all, but Johnny Dollar, Gunsmoke, The Green Hornet, Sam Spade, Hopalong Cassidy, the Cisco Kid, Sid Caesar and Imogine Coca, Gangbusters, Amos and Andy, Our Miss Brooks and Jack Benny were my favorites.

Before we had a TV dad would take us to the Knights of Columbus Hall at the corner of Ridge Road and Rosary Avenue. There was a small TV in the bar area. We would watch two programs, first, *Kookla, Fran and Ollie*, a puppet show with a human host. The host was Fran Allison, and she played the foil to the mischievous Kookla and Ollie. I loved it. The characters were always getting into trouble, especially Ollie (who looked a little like a crocodile) and was not the smart one of the pair. There were other characters who would appear from time to time. The male counterpart to Fran was Burr Tillstrom. He was the main puppeteer.

The other show was *Life is Worth Living*, with Bishop Fulton J. Sheen. Even as a very young person this man held my attention even when I did not know what he was talking about.

Dad was always happy to take us or just me since he enjoyed having a drink as well as the TV shows. The bartender was our next-door neighbor, Tim O'Leary. Tim was one of the nicest people I have ever met in my entire life. He was gentle and strong at the same time and always an Irish twinkle in his eye. There would be a Birch Beer waiting for me on each visit.

Street Name Origins

Who built the houses on Colton, Victory, Crescent and Leo? You might have caught the address of the K of C being on the corner of Rosary Avenue. The name alone, recalls a religious theme. Well, there was a religious theme to the streets in our neighborhood. Starting with Colton Ave., which was named after Bishop Charles H. Colton (1903-1915). Victory Avenue obviously named after Our Lady of Victory. The streets all predate the building of the basilica. Crescent is a symbol used in conjunction with devotion to the Blessed Mother Mary. Leo is for Pope Leo XIII, who was Pope from 1878 to 1903.

According to Mary Hanley and my father, the houses on Victory, Colton, Leo, and Crescent were mostly built and financed by Father Baker, to give Catholic working families a decent place to live. Our house still had the fixtures for gas lighting so it could have predated general use of electricity. Mary Hanley often would tell me about, how as a little girl she would take the mortgage payment to the OLV Rectory and pay it directly to Father Baker. She remembered him fondly. She was in the inaugural First Communion Class at the Basilica. Her stories about Father Baker always held a bit about when Father Baker would visit a classroom at OLV Academy and how he would give each student a piece of candy. They loved his visits. Mary always spoke with reverence when talking about Father Baker, as if he were something well beyond an ordinary priest or person.

The Hanley Family

Mary and her mom would take me to a summer cottage they rented each year in Angola, NY along the shores of Lake Erie. My main memory from these weeklong stays was the breakfasts that Mrs. Hanley would cook for me. Fried eggs cooked in bacon fat would smell and taste so good. No one thought about clogged arteries back then. Oh! How I miss those wonderful eggs.

Mrs. Hanley's first name was Brigid. She would die in 1975 long after I was married and had two children. It just so happened that my third daughter would be born in 1975 and would be three days without a name until we eventually came to agree on Brigid in memory of Mrs. Hanley who had been so kind to me and the story of St. Brigid who is the second favorite saint in Ireland, St. Patrick being the first.

Mary's story does not have a happy ending. She would outlast all her family and would live in the family home by herself for years. I would have work in Buffalo, and I would stay with her usually taking her out to dinner and keeping her company. There was, a period that she became a recluse to the point of not letting me into the house. Eventually she got a little better, but her condition eventually deteriorated to such an extent that she had to be taken to a Nursing Home. She would live there for about four years, but her mind was always back at 69 Colton. I would visit on every business trip. She always knew who I was as if I was a triggering mechanism to transport her back to the time of her family being together. She would tell me that she had to make dinner for the boys, meaning her brothers, who were all long dead. It was so sad to watch this vibrant woman lapse into a shell of her former self. Mary had been active in Democratic Politics and served on the board of Governors of Erie County Community College.

One of my favorite stories she would tell was about the time she and her mom went back to Ireland for a vacation. That would have been in the early fifties. Ireland was not prosperous then and outhouses were still common. She made me laugh with her stories delivered in a brogue that was much accentuated. Not till I was sixty-nine would I enjoy the hospitality of Ireland for myself. It looked and felt nothing like Mary had described. Her version was more like John Wayne's, "The Quiet Man."

Death of a Giant

On August 16, 1948, I saw my dad cry for the first time. I remember him coming into the bedroom I shared with Fran. He was visibly shaken, and tears were coming down his cheek. I asked, "Dad what is the matter?" All he said was, "the Babe died." Of course, I knew exactly what he meant. In our bedroom was a sports calendar and that month it featured a long retired but still, much loved Babe Ruth. That day and that scene has stayed so clear to me all these years.

Dad's Love of Sports

My dad had much to do with my love of sports. He never tired of playing catch with me in front of the house. We would stand twenty feet apart and I would throw a fastball to him as hard as I could. I marveled at how he never had to use a mitt to catch my "powerful throws." This routine would become an after-dinner ritual for dad and me. He would encourage me to play baseball at every level until I stopped playing in high school. Basketball would replace baseball as my passion sport.

Dad was responsible for that switch also. It was the winter of 1949 when dad and his best buddy Eddie O'Hara took me to my first basketball game. The Canisius Golden Griffins were playing Notre Dame at Buffalo's Memorial Auditorium. I remember the crowds more than anything. Back then Canisius played in a double header every Saturday during basketball season and crowds of over 12,000 were the norm. I just remember the excitement as the crowd roared with each basket by the home team. Little did I or my dad know that I would get to play on the same court eleven years into the future? Canisius would go on to win that game 53 to 50 and I was hooked. After that first game, and for many years later Dad and I would go to the Aud, as it was called, every Saturday night. This routine would continue until I enrolled at Niagara University, and he would then come up to Niagara on Saturday nights to see the Purple Eagles play. We would see wonderful basketball and some of the greatest players who ever played the game. I can still picture a lanky kid from West Virginia who seemed to play so effortlessly, yet so effectively. That player was Jerry West.

The one night I will never forget was a game between

Niagara (part of the double header) and Holy Cross, with its national consensus All American Tom Heinsohn at the Aud, February 5th, 1955. There was a bench clearing brawl that had all the fans on their feet for what seemed forever. The contest went back and forth until Niagara pulled away 72 to 68. I could not stop thinking about that game. I remember going to school the following Monday morning and the game was all I could talk about. That was the most exciting game I have ever seen. Holy Cross was ranked 14th in the nation while Niagara was unranked. If the Canisius vs. Notre Dame game I mentioned hooked me, then this one certainly sealed the deal.

One other game stood out in my childhood memory and that was Canisius vs. Duquesne sometime in the early sixties. Willie Somerset from Duquesne would set an Aud scoring record that night with forty plus points. He was only 5' 8" but he could shoot the lights out in the pre-three-point basket era.

One other game I attended was at the Connecticut Street Armory in 1954. Buffalo State was playing Rio Grande College of Ohio. That year Rio Grande had a player that was making national news. His name was Bevo Francis. He already scored over a 100-points in two games and was leading the country in college scoring. Bevo was 6' 9" and a prolific scorer and a consensus All American. Rio Grande would win the game. After I walked up to Bevo and was amazed, as I had never seen anyone that tall.

Often St. Bonaventure would play in the doubleheader instead of Niagara. About the time I was in seventh and eighth grade the Bonnie's had a star player named Brendan McCann. He had a great ability to make blind passes and was a good shot. Well, I took to imitating his every move. I passed like him and I shot like him. Of course, the similarity in our names had a lot to do with it. He was my hero.

Years later my daughters Kelly and Casey would compete in the New York State Empire Games in Lake Placid. My wife and I would be off-ice officials for those games for three years. By doing that we had our accommodations provided for us. One year we were to stay at the Howard Johnson's just outside of the Village of Lake Placid. When I went to register the clerk just gave me a key and said the room was already. Upon entering the room, we found someone else's luggage there. It turned out that my childhood hero Brendan McCann was the Director of the Empire State Winter Games, and he was staying at the same hotel. If fact, it was his room that the clerk mistakenly sent us.

Going to dinner that night, I found myself sitting at a table next to Brendan McCann. I was beside myself. He was only four or five years older than me. I went up to his table and explained the room mix up. Then I went on to tell him how much I worshipped him as an eighth grader. He was embarrassed but so nice about it. We had a very congenial conversation and even speculated on the possibility that we were related.

This episode is just another example how dreams and fantasies can sometimes become real.

Victory Gardens

World War II brought changes to the Home Front. None more visible than the need for Victory Gardens. Families were encouraged to grow their own vegetables so that farmers

55

could concentrate on food for the soldiers fighting the war. Even though the war was over by the time this narrative begins, the McCann's and the O'Leary's next door had Victory gardens still going. Ours wrapped around our garage with a small space in the back up to the neighbor's fence. It was about four feet wide and the full length of the garage. It continued along O'Leary's fence back to the front of the garage. There were tomatoes and bean plants. Our basement had a fruit closet where all the canned fruit and vegetables would be stored. It was full of things that would not be opened until winter. Canning was a big enterprise with my mom and grandma holding forth with huge pots boiling on the stove and glass jars being filled as fast as they could. Some of those jars would even last beyond the winter. Whenever they were opened it was like bringing summer to our dinner table. Even four- and five-year old's can appreciate the fruits of our parent's labors when it comes from home grown food. Sadly, the Victory Garden did not last more than two years after the War.

Canning and Sister Kathleen

The tradition of canning fruit however lasted well into the fifties. Strawberries, peaches, and apples were favorites of my parents. Olcott, New York is a small town along Lake Ontario, just north of Lockport. The closeness to the lake makes for early springs that prove to be just right for fruit development. Each summer our whole family would drive to Olcott for two reasons. The first was to visit my aunt, Sister Mary Kathleen, a Saint Joseph nun. Born Hannah McCann, she was one of dad's three sisters. The St. Joseph nuns ran a summer camp for girls just outside of Olcott, NY. My cousin Betty would attend this camp. A visit to the camp meant sitting in the kitchen having great treats, while the adults talked. They did an awful lot of talking, never running out of words. The other reason was to pick fruit. August was especially good for Peaches, so that is when we always went to see Sr. Kathleen.

One memory of that kitchen was the strips of plastic hanging from the ceiling that had a sort of glue to trap flies. It was very ugly but effective judging from the number of dead flies on each strip.

Picking Peaches

Can you imagine a better place for a young boy than somewhere you could climb trees and help your father simultaneously? It was great fun and I loved (still do) peaches. Years later I took my then two girls to Olcott to pick peaches. We were visiting my cousin Helen and staying at her house. Oh Yes, we flew to Buffalo from Albany. Here we were with three bushels of peaches to take home. I gave one bushel to Helen. Well, we did what any sensible traveler would do. We combined suitcases and filled the rest with peaches and packing material. I remember John Buchheit just shaking his head as I loaded the peaches into the suitcases. By the time we got home we had suitcases full of bruised peaches. Oh well, I tried.

Back to Sister Kathleen. She would be the matriarch of the family after my aunt Liz died. Everyone looked to her for advice and approval, whether it was about marriage, buying a home or any family controversy. She was the reason I did so well in school. During my first nine years of schooling, nuns of her St. Joseph order taught me. That was a double edge sword. The nuns would never hit me or any of my three cousins that shared grades one thru twelve with me. That said, the other edge was that I was terrified of not doing well because Sr. Kathleen would be the first to hear of it. That was never going to happen. I would not want to have her disappointed in me, ever.

Sister Kathleen's Twenty-fifth Anniversary as a Nun

On August 8, 1948, Sr. Kathleen had been a nun for twenty-five years and the family had a huge celebration in her honor. It took place at Cousin Helen's, and everybody was there. At least six of her eleven siblings were there, along with my uncle's wives and Aunt Liz's husband Barney. Cousins from newborns to returning veterans from the War were also present. I just remember the good times playing with all the cousins and everybody being so happy. The family always had a good time when they got together.

Sr. Kathleen would serve her Order for another twenty-five years, dying in 1973. Her influence on the entire family would be felt for years to come. My cousin Helen would then become the matriarch of the family.

Front row; Aunt Liz, Sister Kathleen, Uncle Tom. Back row; Uncle Ed, Uncle Jim, Uncle John, and my dad at the 25th Anniversary.

Floor, Kevin McCann, Fran McCann with Jimmy McDonnell, Bernie McCann, and Mickey Buchheit.
Seated, Lillian (Kilcoyne) McDonnell holding daughter Kathy McDonnell, Sister Kathleen (Hannah McCann), Betty (Buchheit) Eagan holding Jack McDonnell, Rose (Garvin) McDonnell
Standing, Jean (McCann) Chase, Catherine (McDonnell) Kane, Kathleen (Kane) Crowe held by Eugene McDonnell's first wife, name unknown, Tommy Kane, held by Johnny McDonnell, Ann (McDonnel) Giblin, James McDonnell, and Eugene McDonnell.

Loretta Kraft

One of those cousins attending was my dad's first cousin on his mother's side, Loretta Kraft. Loretta lived in Scranton PA. Her immediate family did not work for the steel mills, so they stayed in Scranton in 1900 when my grandfather moved his family to West Seneca. Loretta would become a fixture in my life, being there for me at each milestone.

There was only one word to adequately describe her and that was "classy." I remember her arrival for Sr. Kathleen's party. She pulled up in this large 1938 Chrysler, fancy as all get out. She stepped out of the car dressed in what can only be described as "going out dancing dress." Loretta lived at 708 Crown Avenue in Scranton her entire life which would span over ninety-four years. Mom would take us to Scranton on the Lehigh Valley Train. I remember sleeping in the Pullman Train Car on one trip. What an adventure for a little kid.

Mom and Loretta were pals, more like sisters. They really liked each other as Loretta would recount to me through the years. Her house was a one family, with one bathroom at the top of twenty-two stairs. There was no television until years later. The front porch was my favorite, at least in the summertime. As a youngster I would play out there for hours. As an adult, I would read and nap there for hours. Her kitchen was big and cozy at the same time. In one corner was an old rocking chair with fine filigree all over it. Many a time I would be held by mom or dad and rocked to sleep in that chair. When Loretta died, I was asked if I wanted anything from her house, and I said, "the rocking chair." It graces my home to this day. It must be at least one hundred and fifty years old, as it had belonged to her mom before her. We would visit Scranton as a family at Easter for years. The memories are all sugar coated with wonderful smells from the kitchen and soft breezes on the porch.

Loretta's story was interesting. She first worked for the Scranton Trolley Company in the office. Later in her career she worked as a secretary to Fred Warring, the big band leader. Warring's Band and Choral group, called the Pennsylvanians, would grace the airways with their smooth sound for six decades. Later she worked at Cornell University for years. Her long retirement was filled with friends, travel, and family. She lived alone in that big house but somehow, she never seemed alone. There was her cousin Margaret and husband Charlie who lived across the street and were at 708 every time I arrived. Her best friend Joan Davis was a constant companion. Joan, also a relative, was a buyer for one of the bigger Five and Dime Stores, either Woolworths or Kresge's. She traveled, but always seemed to be there when I arrived. She lived down the street from Loretta.

We will pick up Loretta's story and her influence on me as our story progresses.

Thunderstorms

A frequent visitor to our street, especially in the summertime were the Thunderstorms cascading, with a fury off Lake Erie. I remember one storm when my mom came rushing into the backyard where I was playing by myself. She grabbed me up and carried me into the house to her bedroom. She held me tight as the storm grew more intense. She would shudder nervously with each boom of thunder and crack of lightning. I really did not understand her fright as I thought this was cool as the day turned dark with flashes of lightening strobing across the sky followed by tremendous booms of thunder. Dad always told me that the angels were having a party and that the thunder was just them rolling kegs of beer down the heavenly hallways. I think mom felt it had something to do with the devil rather than angels. I did not inherit her fear. In fact, many a time I would sit on our front porch and watch approaching storms with delight. I would stay on the porch during the storm unless the rain came from the west which would blow right onto the porch. To this day, I still look forward with anticipation to thunderstorms. With each storm I am thrown back to the day mom held me in her arms and pleaded with God to end the storm.

My World Expands

As I got a little older, my world would expand into the large field at the foot of our street. Once in the "field," as we called it, we were far from the watchful eyes of the parents on the street. At first, I could only go if Fran took me, which he reluctantly did at times. At the end of the field which was nothing more than overgrown grass about two feet high at mid-summer, was Smokes Creek. Named for a Seneca tribe member, who lived in the vicinity many years ago and was a very influential person among his people. The creek would flow east to west emptying into Lake Erie somewhere inside of the steel plant grounds. Before it reached the plant it was relatively clean. Fish could be seen if not caught. The creek would have endless fascination for a young boy. It was never very deep, except when jammed with ice. Then it would cause great flooding all along South Park Avenue. Normally, you could walk across it but that never seemed right as wet sneakers would be a big giveaway to where we had been. So, crossing the creek was done by stepping on rocks and stones perfectly placed so that little feet and legs could move from one stone to another until safely on the southern shore, no more than twenty feet away. The best place to cross was near the bridge on South Park Avenue just below Victory Playground.

*Smokes Creek at South Park Bridge near Victory Playground
At Flood Stage January 1959. My photo.*

Going under that bridge was also a big thing for a little boy. Who knew what hobos were staying there just waiting for an unsuspecting little boy to come along? At least, that is what our parents told us. We never saw any and therefore did not worry about it. I found it a place where I could sit and think about things and maybe even pray.

Bob and I, and sometimes Larry Butler would spend hours playing in and around this magical creek with the funny name.

In the winter, as I got older the creek and its surrounding ponds and streams would be our skating venue. Across South Park was another field which we called the "big field." It had a stream running through it starting at Cemetery Pond to the Mud Hole on to Smokes Creek. It was ready made for a skating adventure.

Cemetery Pond, named for its proximity to Old Holy Cross Cemetery, was perfect for Pond Hockey. The bigger boys would start a fire near the Pond where you could put your skates on. The skates I used were not exactly mine. Fran and I had a pair between us. To make them fit, I had to fill the void with loose newspaper. I was not the graceful skater I envisioned in my mind with skates three sizes too big, but I had fun nevertheless. Sometimes we would skate along the streams, but we had to be more careful, as the ice did not thicken up like the pond.

The field seemed to go on forever. That was because I was not allowed to go past the cemetery. Early on I could only go if Fran was with me. Those limitations would dissolve with the years and my exploring would extend all the way to the railroad tracks of the Lehigh Valley Line, a single-track leaving Buffalo and heading southeast. Bob and I would sometimes walk up to the track around three in the afternoon when a train usually went by. For some strange reason we would yell at the engineer to throw us a flare. He never did but we were always hopeful. The tracks of the LVRR might well have been the Great Wall of China as far as we were concerned because there was no going beyond it. That was still a long way from home for 10- and 11- year-old. Today's children would never be allowed to go that far from home.

Mom's Death

May 1st in Lackawanna of 1952, May Day, was full of religious ceremonies. In the evening there was always a procession from the Basilica to a vacant lot next to the American Legion Hall on Ridge Road. There, one of the girls would have the honor of crowning a statue of Mary with a crown of flowers. We would practice the May Day songs for weeks before the big day. It was a purely happy occasion with deep religious overtones. This would be my third May Day procession, as I was in the third grade and Miss Hagel was my teacher. I am pretty sure she was a first-year teacher. Even to an eight-year-old she appeared to be young.

The story of that May Day should really start a year before. My mom had developed a growth on her neck. I called it a growth, while it was really a cancerous tumor the size of a baseball. I know dad and she were very worried. There were trips to the hospital for radiation treatments at Roswell Park Cancer Institute. Dad's sister-in-law, my Aunt Betty, had a brother Dr. John O'Brien, who was a cancer specialist and therefore mom's doctor. I distinctly remember the day she came home from the hospital and the growth was gone. She had bandages around her neck but a smile on her face. I thanked God that day.

Unfortunately, the cancer had spread to other parts of her body. For the next nine months dad would take her to the Roswell Park Hospital in Buffalo for increased radiation treatments. Mom was getting smaller and thinner every day. Her

VISITORS TO MY STREET

faith however, continued to grow. She prayed for a miracle that would never come.

One day I particularly remember she was having Club, as the ladies called it. They were five or six women who all taught school with her. They would meet once a month at one of their homes and have tea, cake, and talk. They may have played cards for all I knew. All I can really remember was that when it was mom's turn to have Club, the house would get a scrubbing down like no other. These women would be her best friends and they were more like family than just co-workers.

On that Club Day the women were in the living room. I was in the kitchen by myself. They could see me, but they were not paying attention to a cute eight-year-old. I, in the meantime, was taking ingredients from the spice rack, added flour, sugar, and anything else I could pore into a big yellow mixing bowl. I stirred it and was about to turn on the oven when mom came out and asked what I was doing. That is when I said, "I am making a mixture for you to drink that will cure your cancer." She started crying while hugging me as tight as I had ever been hugged. She quickly cleaned up the mess I made and sent me upstairs to play.

On Valentine's Day 1952, I was at school having a class party where we exchanged Valentines with our classmates. The Principal, Sister De LaSalle came to the door and spoke to Miss Hagel very quietly. Miss Hagel called my name, and I went up to her. She just said that I had to go home as my mom was not doing well. She said my dad wanted me home. My classmates stopped what they were doing and just watched as I collected my things and walked out the door. This was about 2:30 in the afternoon. I had just been home for lunch at 12:30. Back then we went home every day for lunch unless you lived a certain distance from the school.

I remember that walk as being the longest walk I ever remembered. My mind was full of all sorts of not good scenarios. When I reached home, everyone was in her bedroom arranged around her bed. Mom looked so small and frail. Fran had gotten home before me and just came up to me and put his arm around me. Monsignor Joseph Maguire came in moments later. He started giving mom the Last Rites of the Church. Having been taught in school what that was all about, I became very frightened. When all the prayers were over and the Monsignor had left, mom seemed more at ease. As I recall she slept the rest of the day. I played outside or in the basement. When dad put us to bed, he asked us to pray extra hard for mom. Mom was still with us in the morning, and I could not have been happier. They did teach us in school about Extreme Unction and that sometimes it helped people to recover. That was February 14th and mom would still be with us up until that May Day celebration I mentioned.

After the ceremony at the Legion Field, I came home and was told to play outside until dark. It was a Thursday night. My best friend Ozzie from across the street was always up for a game of catch. He was three years older than me, but we loved to play all sorts of sports games with each other. That night we played catch with a football. The object of our game was to throw the ball over the head of the other guy. If you caught the ball the other guy could not move until you threw the ball. We would play this game endlessly and for years.

When darkness fell, I was called in just like the other children who were being called by their parents. Little did I know that was the last night I would have my mother. As I write these words it is May 1st, 2019, sixty-seven years later. The pain has not diminished, the loss felt just as strongly. Mom was sleeping when I went in, so I went right off to bed.

The next thing I know Dad is waking Fran and me and told us our mother had passed away during the night. I thought I was dreaming, a very bad dream. For years I was living inside of a bad dream and that someday I would wake up and mom would still be with us. I never woke up from that dream and would live the rest of my life inside that horrible dream.

Dad suggested we both get dressed and go to church for morning mass. It was First Friday, a significant day in the Liturgical Calendar. Throughout grammar school the entire school would always go to mass on First Fridays before the start of classes and we would have a small breakfast in the cafeteria afterwards.

I paid little attention to the mass. My little mind was twirling with thoughts of dreams and sorrow deeper than I have ever felt before or since. Mom had been a paragon of strength. Her faith in God and the goodness of her fellow man kept her able to deal with any situation. As a family, every day in Lent, we would kneel around the bed and say the Rosary. Her Rosary was never far from her reach. She was so devoted to God and her family. I know she worried what would happen to Fran and me. I just wish I had five minutes to tell her we did OK and that she had five beautiful and wonderful granddaughters and five wonderful great grandchildren. She was only 41 years old.

By the time we got home and had a little breakfast, things started happening at the house. Relatives started to arrive with Helen Buchheit taking charge. The house would be cleaned from top to bottom. Furniture was moved out of the living room to make space for the casket that arrived later in the day. On towards five O'clock that big 1938 Chrysler pulled up to our curb and out stepped Loretta. She had driven all the way from Scranton as soon as she heard the news. I am sure my dad called her as they were more like siblings than first cousins. They grew up in the same house as their families lived together for a time in Scranton.

Loretta was distraught but nevertheless took time to try to console Fran and me. She would be my rock for decades yet to come.

With all the activity going on and not much for a little boy in the depths of sadness to do, my uncle Art gave me a dollar and said go buy baseball cards. My collection of baseball cards was already quite large and a whole dollars' worth would make it even better. So off to the corner store on Electric Avenue (one street over) I would go. When I walked into the store, I was immediately met by Mrs. Witerski, the owner along with her husband. She somehow already knew about mom's death. Now Mrs. Witurski was never a friendly person, in fact, Mrs. Olsen from Little House on the Prairie reminds me of her. But her sorrow for me that day was so genuine that I was moved to hug her.

Being Friday, my friends were all in school. I had to wait for what seemed like hours for Davy Guarino to come home. Mrs. Guarino came over when she got home from school. She and mom were both teachers and would often walk home together. Her children were like siblings to me. Dave and I talked and cried together along with Mary, his older sister. Dave would be my best friend all my life. His sister, Mary, was the sister I never had.

The rest of the day was a blur. I do not remember eating but I must have, as food kept arriving in prodigious amounts from neighbors, friends, and relatives. My Uncle Fee, mom's brother and his wife, my aunt Peg would arrive in the evening from Corning. They were my God parents and would be very special to me for the rest of their lives.

I do not know when the casket arrived but if must have been either Friday night or early Saturday morning. The Wake would go on for two whole days. People came in an unending stream. Fellow teachers, clergy, nuns, neighbors, relatives and so many of mom's students would come to pay their respects. They all loved her. She was so kind and gentle with everyone. Never said a mean word about anyone. Her devotion to her students was remarkable. Even in her sickness she made every effort to be in class as much as she could. Every student was special to her, and they all knew it. Mom taught Business at Lackawanna High School. To this day the school still gives the Catherine McCann Award to a deserving student. For years after I would meet people who knew mom and they would all relate to me what a wonderful person she was.

That night sleep came hard. With furniture moved, much of it ended up in our bedroom so things were vastly out of sorts. For the next two nights there was noise of conversations coming from the kitchen. This was an Irish Wake where relatives and friends would stay awake all night with the deceased. My uncles and cousins were downstairs having a drink on my mom's behalf. I do not know how they or my dad functioned over the next few days. I was still in my bad dream mode and would be for many years. The flower arrangement on the front door told people that a Wake was in progress. The whole neighborhood was in mourning. Kids stopped playing, at least, anywhere near our house. Most, if not all, my friends would come in to give their condolences. I do remember that they all came dressed up for such an occasion. All my teachers and Fran's teachers showed up. Many of my relatives still lived in the Buffalo area so they were among the constant stream of mourners.

I do not remember much about what my grandmother,

who had lost a daughter, was doing. It must have been very hard on her. She was 68 years old, a widow and living with her daughter who was now gone. Somewhere along the way dad would let her know that she was welcome to stay if she wanted. Their relationship was not always congenial, to say the least. I would become the object of her attention after mom died. That meant I had to go with her wherever she went unless her sons Art and John took her.

The Wake never let up for lack of visitors. The all-night routine would spill over to Sunday night. I dreaded the funeral. That last night of the Wake I went up to the casket and touched my mom on the face. She was so cold and hard, not the soft warm person who comforted me when I scraped my knees so often. Being so young I had a hard time processing that change. How could that be my mom? What was life in heaven for her likely to be? Was she watching me right now? All these thoughts and more were running through my head and just making matters so much harder for me. During the two days of the Wake, I did not talk much with anyone, except Davy. I kept my thoughts, worries and fears to myself.

The day of the funeral came on a beautiful Monday in May. Today they call it Cinco De Mayo. The procession from Colton to the Basilica was a short two blocks yet there were so many cars it took some time. My first cousin Tom Cusack was the Funeral Director. It was the first funeral for his business. His son Mike followed in his footsteps. Tommy was my Aunt Mary McCann's son. Her story will have to follow. She was not at the funeral because she lived in California.

Going into the Basilica right behind the casket dad was holding on to both Fran and me. As we went down the aisle, I was struck by all the eyes looking at us. There was not an empty seat in the church which holds about two thousand people. Our whole grammar school was there, the senior class from Lackawanna High School, the Sisters of Saint Joseph, about everyone who attended the Wake also came to the funeral. I mostly remember not crying. My tears had been all used up over the last few days. I do not know why, but I thought it important not to cry. I think it may have been I was worried if dad saw me cry that it would be too much for him to take. So, I guess I did it for him. His pain must have been unimaginable. Later in life I learned that mom was the second woman in his life

Before dad met mom he had been engaged to another woman. Her name was Alice Galligan. Her sister Pauline lived on our street and years later she would tell me how dad had cared for her sister. Alice died before they could get married. All I know is that she suffered from Rheumatoid Arthritis or another such debilitating illness. She was house bound for a long time. Her sister Pauline Alcott told me she remembered my dad carrying her sister to the car and then taking her for appointments. Her niece, Pat Galligan, told the family story about her aunt. That Alice once worked for Father Baker as a secretary. One day Father Baker came to see her at home. He said to Alice that she has been suffering for a long time. He would go home and pray to the Blessed Mother for her. Alice died that night. Her family felt and still feels that it was a miracle that her suffering was relieved.

The effect on my father must have been profound. I am sure the two deaths now played hard on dad, as he was never the same person after mom died. The prankster and joker he had been, was no more. He was serious and quiet. He spent more time at the K of C bar. My heart would ache for him although I did not have a clue of the depths of his sadness.

The mass was a blur, as had much of the last few days

had been. The procession to the graveyard was long and slow. Mom would be buried in the "new" section of Holy Cross Cemetery. What is highlighted in my memory is the last act before the casket was lowered. Dad, Fran, and I stood next to the casket as it was being lowered and each of us was expected to drop dirt on the casket. As I dropped my little handful into the grave, I felt like I was hurting mom. It took the dirt a long time, in my mind, to reach the casket. I can hear the noise it made even today. That final act ending a three-day long process of grief, prayer, hoping to wake up, and just being so sad. My mom was gone, and life had to continue. I look back with solace that so many people loved my mom. None more than me or Dad or Fran. Yet it was and is heartening to know she lived her short life with such grace, dignity, and strength. Dad would often say that she never complained no matter how much she was suffering. Her only lament was worry for me and Fran and what would become of us.

Those years right after mom died were terrible. I kept hoping I would wake up and those last few years would have been just a bad dream. That expectant feeling lasted for much of my early life. Now that I am so much older than she ever was, I know it was not a dream. Dreams could never hurt that much.

Clean Floors

The routine of daily life on Colton Avenue is fixed in my mind. The ordinary things people do stand out to me as important markers of life. One such event which repeated itself about once every two weeks was the cleaning and waxing of the linoleum floors in the kitchen and downstairs hallway. Our house was a two story with an attic as the third. We used the front door or the porch entrance only in summer. Everybody came in the side door from the driveway. You could go directly to the basement or go up to the first floor or then continue up to the second floor. Usually on a Thursday when I came home from school, I was greeted with the floors covered with newspapers. That was because Gramma had washed and waxed the floors and you needed to walk carefully around, thus the newspapers. They would only be down until suppertime and then the house would go back to normal.

Local Dairy

Just around the corner on Electric Ave. was the Beres Dairy. You could hear bottles clinking all the time. They had the best Chocolate Milk I have ever tasted. For years when I came back to Lackawanna I would stop and buy a quart of Chocolate Milk.

Leaves

One of the big annual events was the falling of the leaves. As I mentioned each house had at least two trees guarding it. Next door at O'Leary's they had a monstrous Elm tree that rose to heights higher than the house. It rained leaves and more leaves, and they did not all land on O'Leary's property.

So large piles would be raked, and hours spent jumping into them. We would devise all sorts of games with the leaves, but the main function of the raking was to form large piles in the street next to the curb. Dad would then supervise the lighting of the pile. Fran or I was left to control the fire making sure it did not get out of hand. Imagine if you can, fires all along the street with smoke going everywhere. If the TV antenna wave lengths did not get me imagine the tons of carcinogens of smoke inhaled from those leaves.

Sledding

Wintertime meant sledding on our American Flyer Sleds. The northern terminus of Colton Avenue is on Ridge Road. There is a ridge that slopes down toward Smokes Creek. That makes Colton a hill, at least for the block nearest Ridge. That would give us kids advantages. The first was a great place to sleigh ride starting at the top at Ridge Road and continuing, if you were good, to Crescent Street where the road started to level off. In the 1940's Colton was a two-way street with few cars traversing in either direction. Once the morning visitors had come and gone there would be little traffic till the men came home and not much then because few had cars. That left the road open to daredevil's belly flopping for all they were worth. What a sensation to be tearing down the hill right at ground level with your earflaps slapping at your head. There was always someone coming up the hill for their next run and they would warn you of any cars coming. The good sleighing would only last a day as the plows would eventually destroy our downhill course.

One "sport" the older kids participated in was "hopping a car." At a stop sign they would wait for a car to come to a stop and then sneak behind the car and bend down and grab the rear fender. When the car accelerated the boys would hold on for as long as they dared before letting go. Not very smart in retrospect, and I never did it. Dad would have killed me if I did that.

As the fifties came along the streets were changed to one-way thoroughfares with Colton going up to Ridge and Victory coming down. With more cars on the road and the one-way direction came the end of sleigh riding on Colton.

When the street gained traffic there was never enough snow on it to allow for good sledding. We then moved to Crosta's small hill near their garage. That was tricky because you had to make a 180 degree turn from the garage to the yard. As we got older and could range further from home we moved to South Park near the Botanical Conservatory. Just a small hill but a fast descent. One day while sledding there I somehow ripped my pants leaving an embarrassing gap in them. That was a long walk home all the time trying to hide the hole.

Winter in Western New York meant you started wearing your winter boots. These black rubber boots went right over your shoes. They had metal clasps that tightened to your foot. It was years later that the clasps were replaced by sippers. Our parents made us put an empty bread bag over our shoes to make sure the shoes never got wet. The plastic bag also made it easier to put on the boots.

Hydraulic Engineers

The slight hill on Colton also made for a virtual river coming down along the curb when the snow started to melt in the springtime. We would become water diversion engineers. Bob, Dave, and I would build dams with snow to plug up the mainstream and then divert it into intricately designed smaller streams. We got wet and the motorists did not always appreciate our engineering skills. If anyone complained, we merely broke the dam, and the water would flow in its usual course. This activity gave us hours of pleasure and I am sure it helped with our imagination development.

Love of Flowers

Speaking of spring my thoughts go to the backyard and of the array of flowers my mom transplanted from her home in Corning New York. Mom loved her flowers, and I would continue that love till this day. She had a rock garden just below the kitchen window so she could peer out any time to enjoy nature's handy work. The rock garden featured Pansies, Iris, Bleeding Hearts, Peonies, and my favorite Morning Glories. It was my job to count the Morning Glory flowers each day. They were a most beautiful sky-blue color. Along the side of the house, she would plant Pansies every year and Lilies of the Valley came up annually. Our yard was small, but mom made it look beautiful and it taught me to appreciate beauty in all forms.

Roller-skating

Springtime also brought out the roller skates. We would be out on the sidewalks as soon as the snow was off them. Colton and Victory being hills allowed for downhill runs on skates. It also made for going too fast and consequent falls and skinned knees. I was perpetually with scabs on my knees. We would have a skate key for tightening and loosening the skates hanging around the necks.

Go Fly a Kite

Mid-March would be a time for kites. They would be homemade paper kites. Old rags made up the tail. A vacant lot at the corner of Colton and Maple Grove would be full of children flying their special kites. It was always fun, but the flimsy kites usually did not last long. As we grew older cloth kites would replace the paper ones.

When the weather was not conducive to outdoor play our attic was the go-to place. The attic was cavernous and mysterious. The entrance was on the second floor through a door in the hallway. The hallway also led to the four bedrooms and the only bathroom in the house. The attic door was always closed due to the fact it was not heated. The stairway up was forever dark with only a bare lightbulb for illumination.

The Attic

The attic was my indoor playground. Gramma and dad never came up there. They would just yell from the bottom of the stairs for me to come to dinner or whatever. It was too cold in the winter and awful hot in the summer. But spring and fall were perfect and that is when I played with my Fort Apache set or my military ships. Joe Underiner, mom's godfather, gave Fran and me a steel set of the World War One American Naval Fleet. I have no idea whatever became of them, but they were wonderful. Each ship had wheels on the bottom and were about four or five inches long. I would maneuver those ships for what seemed like hours. They were mostly battleships and destroyers. I would arrange them in various formations and do pretend engagements with pretend enemies. Their features were so realistic that with a vibrant imagination they could become real.

Fort Apache was made of metal that clicked together. I kept mine always set up. I had lots of plastic horses and cowboys, as well as cavalry soldiers on horseback. The soldiers in the Fort would sometimes venture out to repel invading enemies. I also had a Lincoln Logs set that I would build and rebuild log cabins with.

The floors were covered by large rugs that used to grace our living and dining room. Dad had wall to wall carpets installed and I become the beneficiary of nice carpets for my playland.

Sometimes Bob, Davey and I would play hide and seek with the lights out in the attic. There was so much stuff, from old trunks to standup clothes cabinets to hide in and around. It also had a certain smell of old things no longer used by people. I found that to be a sad thing since the treasures I found there would have at one time made some person happy. Now they just sit and wait for me to play with them.

The attic was my own realm. It was a safe place with memories surrounding me. There were things of my mom still there. There were winter clothes or summer clothes packed away in moth balls. The only downside to the attic was the lighting. Only two bare bulbs provided illumination along with a small window at each end of the attic. Still, it was my haven. No noise from the house below could penetrate its beams. We all need our little space where we can sit back and be with ourselves. The company is always good.

Chestnut Ridge Picnics

The County of Erie has a wonderful Park System, with Chestnut Ridge Park being the crown jewel. Located south of Orchard Park it has two large toboggan runs. (There were three when I was young) There is also, the ever enchanting, One Hundred Steps taking you down to Eighteen Mile Run Creek. In addition, there are tennis courts and hundreds of wonderful picnic sites. My very early memories are of those picnic sites with mom and dad, later with the Altar Boys and even later as the place for years of McCann/McDonnell Family Reunions. This place holds precious memories for thousands of Western New Yorkers.

As a little kid my first slide, swings, and the dizzying merry go round were experienced at Chestnut Ridge. I can still see my mom spreading the tablecloth on the picnic table and putting out our lunch. Exactly why that is magical I cannot express in words. Maybe it was the summer warmth, along with mom and dad being relaxed and happy. Here was a couple who were always dressed up. Only in his advanced years did dad ever wear a short sleeve shirt or khaki pants. Growing up he was always in dress slacks coat and tie. Mom likewise was always in a nice dress and always a hat. Maybe it was their profession as teachers that they had to meet a certain image. My wife thinks I inherited that trait. Their style of being "dressed up" is certainly lacking in today's world.

Football

Dick Hanley's yard football. The Hanley (down the street as opposed to the Hanley's across the street) yard was the narrowest on the street. They shared a driveway and garage with the McCabe's next store and that took part their backyard away. Even with a 10 – 12 feet wide yard we were always able to get a game of touch football in play. Dick, a year older, would become a starting halfback on our school football team. The group, including Bobby Buchheit, both Haggerty's, Larry Butler, Dave Guarino, Dick, and I would play in that diminutive arena every fall.

Across the street was McGuire's yard which was much longer and wider. We could only play there if Mrs. McGuire's grandson, Mike Franey was playing. Therefore, we always let him play. This yard would be the site of epic football battles. Sometimes we would even wear helmets. Not the super hard plastic ones of today but the softer leather helmets that did little to protect you but also did little harm to opponents. Teams were always chosen via the oldest two taking turns choosing who would be on their team. We would do the "odd or even" game to decide who chose first. (You would each throw out a certain number of fingers and if the total number were odd or even then you would win if that was your choice.) Nobody was left out of a game even if one team had more players.

Nobody ever seemed to get hurt. We all knew that you played within certain restraints so no one would get hurt. We all liked each other and would never want to hurt one another. We were more than friends. We were part of a neighborhood of children who looked out for each other, cared for each other because we were all part of each other's lives. They were part of your daily play time. They were the ones who picked you up when you were down. They were your constant companions. There was no escape to a Game Boy, XBOX, or phone. You simply could not be alone in that neighborhood. Someone was always there to play with you.

You may just stay at Dick's for lunch because Mrs. Hanley was always kind to us. She was another parent who always was "dressed to the nines." I do not remember what Mr. Hanley did for a living but they always had a nice car, a big Hudson. Other mothers who did not work would have house dresses on during the day. This was the dress one wore when doing housework. Never, ever, would a woman wear her housedress outside the house. It just was not done. When the men got home usually the house dress was exchanged for something more appropriate for supper and later in the evening for listening to the radio or in later years, watching TV.

Mothers on the Street

There was an interesting divide between the mothers who worked and those who stayed home. There were few working mothers on the street. My mom, Mrs. Guarino and Mrs. Shea were all schoolteachers at Lackawanna High, Mrs. Merrick was the head librarian at the library. They would be, "dressed to the nines" each morning but would change into house dresses or house coats worn over their better dresses when they got home from work. That way they would not soil their better wear while fixing dinner. Mom did not have to worry about dinner because her mom lived with us and did that chore. Mrs. Guarino had a maid, Zelia Yerry, who had dinner ready for that household. I do not know what the Shea's did, as I was never there for dinner. I was at Guarino's often.

Zelia Yerry, was a live-in maid. She was a simple soul who was tasked with watching out for the children as well as the domestic chores. She left the house very infrequently. She talked little, but you could tell she loved the three Guarino children, as if they were her own. I dare say she felt the same about me, especially after my mom died.

Zelia had a sister, Eva, who would visit sometimes. Eva invited my parents to bring Fran and me to their home in the Catskill Mountains of New York. This would be one of our first trips after the war. They owned a big old farmhouse with a barn and animals. I was very little but do remember the open pastures and the beautiful mountains all around. It still amazes me to this day how kind and generous people were to my mom.

Ross Guarino, Sr.

Mr. Ross Guarino, Sr., owned and ran a gas station (Mobil) and repair shop on South Park Avenue near Maple Grove Avenue. He was one of the most trusted mechanics in Lackawanna. His son Dave would inherit that skill and reputation. Ross was also a man of few words. He was out early and worked long hard hours. He would come home with a day's worth of accumulated grease and grime on himself and his clothes. After changing he would sit in the living room and instantly fall asleep. I never met a man who could work so long and so hard, day in and day out. I remember one day when he was over ninety, I was visiting their cottage in Angola. As I walked down the driveway there was Ross on the roof nailing shingles. My heart was in my throat, but he calmly got on the ladder and came down to greet me. He sounded gruff sometimes, but it was all show. He was the kindest man I knew. He would do anything for you.

The Women of Colton

The mothers who did not work outside the home would be in their house wear all day unless they went out to the store or over to church. If they had little ones at home, lunch was a big deal. Along with naps to be supervised and dinners to prepare and house cleaning and laundry to do, their work was never done. The cleaning was usually divided by a day of the week. For instance, vacuuming would be one day, floors cleaned and waxed another. Dusting was a constant due to the Steel Plant being so close. It was once a week in the winter and more often in warmer weather with the windows open.

The cleaning and waxing of the floors were especially hard work. The linoleum had to be cleaned and then waxed. For Granma that meant Thursdays. Once, every so often, the cleaning required the removal of built-up wax. That took extra time and effort. Then, of course, the floors had to be waxed to protect the shine. Once this was done the floors had to be protected from the ravages of the likes of me. That is why the newspapers were laid out.

My grandmother's day was uniform. She would not get up until mom and dad had gone to school and Fran had left. In the early years I was home alone with her. She would eat breakfast while listening to the Don McNeil Hour. It was a morning show with music, talk, and guests who would appear and perform. One thing that occurred every day during the show as Mr. McNeil talked to the woman listening was his effort to get people up and moving in the morning. He would play marching music and instruct everyone to get up and walk around the breakfast table. Millions of listeners would obey that directive and begin walking around their breakfast tables, Granma and I included. Once the music stopped a second cup of coffee would be had by all. When that show was over she would listen to music from a local station, until the kitchen was picked up. Then she went right into the evening meal preparation. Potatoes and carrots would be pealed, cans opened, and everything was put into pots and pans ready to start cooking. Everything was put in a back hallway that had no heat, so everything stayed cool until time for supper.

Next, she would do whatever that day of the week demanded. If laundry, it was down to the basement. No dryer in those days so after washing the clothes would either go to be hung on the line outside or, if too cold, hung on the lines in the basement. By later in the day the wash would be checked and taken down and folded.

By three in the afternoon, she was sure to have all work completed, except the actual cooking of the supper. She would go to her upstairs rooms (she had a bedroom and a parlor/study). There she would spend the next few hours listening to her "soap operas." Young Doctor Malone, Days of Our Lives, Guiding Light and more, all sponsored by cleaning product manufacturers, hence the name Soap Operas. I would be on her knee also listening.

Family Vacation in Canada

My memories of my mother are few and fleeting. Those that stand out I often revisit in my mind. They comfort me now, since in the memories, I am being comforted. One that stands out took place during a family vacation to Minors Bay Lodge in Ontario, Canada

I remember my cousin Bernard McDonnell talking to dad about this wonderful place north of Toronto. We had just bought our first post-war car, as I mentioned before, and it would be off to Canada that summer.

This lodge is still in existence and from their current website, it looks the same as I remember in 1948. It is nestled in a vast forest on the shore of beautiful Gull Lake. Fran and I had a great time "swimming" and riding in a rowboat. I did not actually swim as I would put my hands on the bottom and bring them up as if I was swimming. I was so proud, and mom was watching and encouraging me. I have often thought how she would have liked all my sports activities through the years. Dad was always there for me though he said very little. Whatever the sport, baseball, basketball, track, cross country, or tennis, I was pretty good at all of them. I think she would have been more vocal than dad. Do not get me wrong, I was happy that dad was not vocal, I never wanted one of those obnoxious parents who yelled at refs and "coached" their kids from the stands. He never did either of those things.

Back to Minors Bay. It was one of those places where the meals are included with the rooms. We had a big room with two double beds and a window. One afternoon I was down by the lake watching men fishing in a rowboat not too far from shore. Suddenly there was a flurry of activity on the boat. They caught something. It turned out to be a large fish (kind unknown). As I watched, one of the men picked up an oar and smashed down on the squiggly fishes' head. That scene stayed in my brain, and I was appalled. I went back to our room, very upset and bothered by what I saw.

That night we went downstairs to the dining room. As the server was taking our orders, just the drinks since you had no choices for the meals. Whatever was being served, that is what you got. She announced that we would be having fish freshly caught that afternoon. I was pretty sure that the fish I saw with its brains bashed in was what was to be on our plates that night. I was full of revulsion and hence no way was I going to eat any of that poor fish. When the server left, I announced that I did not want any fish. Dad, who paid for the vacation did not like that idea. He merely said, "Oh yes you will." At four or five I was rather stubborn and the only confrontation I ever had with my dad took place. Needless to say, I came out the loser. I was taken back up to our room and left there with no dinner. I remember crying, but still happy that I did not have to eat that fish.

It seemed like forever until they all came back. Nobody said anything except my mom. She took me out of the room and down to the snack bar area in the building next door. There she ordered me tea and toast. I can still remember how good the strawberry jam tasted on that toast. She did not scold me, instead she just put her arm around my shoulders as I ate. Words defy how comfortable and calming that made me feel.

Tea and Toast and Holy Communion

Over the next few years until mom was gone, tea and toast would be my comfort food of choice. Once I had made my first communion, every Saturday night we had a routine. The once-a-week bath, followed by time to listen to Gang Busters and the Green Hornet on the radio. While that was on, mom would bring tea and toast to both Fran and me. The idea behind this was that in the morning we could not eat or drink until after mass and Holy Communion. My mom figured this snack would hold us over till breakfast.

That prohibition of not having anything to drink or eat before taking Holy Communion was taken very seriously by the nuns at school. On the day of my own First Communion, we were lined up in the school hallway waiting to process to the Basilica. I was surprised to see every water fountain in the school covered by white cloths. No sneaking a drink in there. I also distinctly remember Sister Perpetua telling the story of a boy from last year's class having taken a sip of water and was thus taken out of line and not allowed to make his First

Communion. Decades later, only five years ago, I was having lunch in Lake Placid with an old school friend, Joe Quinn. We had not seen each other in more than fifty years. Joe was camping in the area with his family, and we got together, thanks to Facebook. Somehow First Communion came up as we were reminiscing about our youth. Turns out Joe was that kid who took that fateful sip of water and was taken out of the line and had to receive his First Communion later. Funny how things come around. I caught up to Joe in seventh grade and we would then spend the next six years in school together. I cherish his friendship to this day. He is a retired, prominent funeral director from the Buffalo area and now enjoys retirement in Florida.

Early Childhood Education

Children get early school experience today by going to Pre-school. No such thing existed in Lackawanna to the best of my knowledge. I, on the other hand, with two teachers for parents had an extensive pre-school experience. Not that I sat in a classroom, but I often went to school. It must have been times when grandma was either sick or away for some reason. Mom or dad would take me to school with them.

Mom was a business teacher at Lackawanna High School, just a short walk from our house. I had to be under five at this time, but certain things stand out. One was that mom taught typing. I remember getting to play on the typewriter and how cool that was for a little kid. I also remember her friends always making a fuss about me. The blackboards were a constant source of amusement. What I did while she was teaching, I just do not remember.

VISITORS TO MY STREET

Dad's school had much more to interest a young person such as myself. Dad was an Industrial Arts teacher at Roosevelt School. It was located on the west side of the Railroad tracks very close to the Steel Plant. It would be my first close contact with African Americans, as many of the students came from African American families.

Also, in the school was my dad's brother Ed. He was the school principal. My experiences included time in his office as well. One memory of his office was the recording machine on his desk. It was one of those big things with two large reels that one would switch on and off as you talked. It was the first time I ever heard my own voice. Pretty exciting for a little boy.

Dad had a busy schedule, so I was sometimes across the hall with the school nurse, Mrs. Coggins, who was a good friend of the family. She would let me sit in the dentist chair and play with the instruments. I told you this was a good preschool experience. I would continue to visit Dad's school after I was in grammar school. Whenever we had a religious Holiday from school, Dad would take me with him.

Dad's classroom was full of tools and clay and other things to play with. When he taught, I would be either sent to Uncle Ed's office or to the gym with dad's good friend, Bill Raid, the gym teacher. It was there I started throwing a ball towards a basket. I was too small to hold a basketball so Bill would give me a volleyball to use instead.

Sometimes dad would have a student "watch" me for a period or so. His name was James Battle. He was a talented artist. I remember him winning a talent contest that my brother Fran was also involved in. Fran got second or third place for a Stamp Collection Display. James got first place for a painting.

Dad's Night School

After my mom died, dad would come home from school about four or four thirty. He would head to the living room and sit in his favorite chair. Sometimes he would read the Buffalo Evening News, which was the afternoon paper, but he never got too far. He would be asleep until supper time.

Three nights a week he would leave for school again as he taught night school. He was a ceramics teacher. Many of the students were woman from Ukraine who had migrated after the war. They did beautiful figurines. Their specialty was making fabulously ornamented colored eggs. Words cannot describe just how beautiful these eggs looked. Dad would bring those eggs home and I kept four of them for many years but alas they are all gone.

No wonder he was tired with that schedule.

I often wondered how he could fall asleep so fast. It was not until I started teaching that I realized why he was so tired. My first year of teaching at age fifty-two found me falling asleep on the way home when I was not driving in my carpool. It was a thirty-minute drive and within five minutes I was out.

Francis "Kelly" McCann

There have been two Kelly McCann's in my family. First, my dad, and now my daughter Kelly, who was named after him. She is a prominent physician in Southern California.

My dad was a wonderful man. He was quiet, yet strong. I marveled at his strength. Whenever we had to fix something, and it required unscrewing a bolt or separating a pipe he would always be able to get it loosened. Despite his strength, his heart was broken and there was little I could do to fix it. I did what I was able and that was to make him as proud of me as I could. In sports, academics or just behavior, I could not afford to see him disappointed. He had had enough of that in his life to defeat any man. Thus, I ran as fast as I could in every race, jumped and scored as much in every game of basketball or pitched as hard as I could in every baseball game. There were hundreds of those games and races over the years. He was my motivation. As I write this at an age of what dad was when he died, I am just now realizing this fact. I always put it down to being ultra-competitive, but it was to make dad proud of me so that he would forget his sorrow even for just a few minutes. I miss you dad.

Back to Colton

On upper Colton lived an elderly woman named, Mrs. Wicks. She had a big house like ours, right next to the Hendra's. I got to know her from the fact she ran a small shop in her basement. You could buy cereal, can goods and I really cannot remember what else she had except "caps." I do not mean hats but caps, for cap guns which every kid on the street had at least one. The early version came in rolls that fit into the gun and you could shoot off the whole roll, if it worked correctly, which it rarely did. The most efficient caps came in a disk with six shots to match our Six Shooters. After all, we were all fans of Hopalong Cassidy, Roy Rogers, The Cisco Kid, and Gene Autry. These were all radio programs we listened to with avid attention. Not to forget Sky King and Sgt. Preston of the RCMP. Our bikes and scooters were our horses, and we all had a gun and holster. That would all be frowned upon today. But in our time and in our imagination, it was natural, and I can assert that no one from Colton Avenue ever became a serial killer. In fact, Ross Guarino was an All-American Rifle team member in college.

I do not remember when Mrs. Wicks closed her little store. I assume it was sometime after I finished using cap guns.

Family Gatherings

Sunday mornings at Aunt Liz's were special. When someone says that family is everything, it makes me think of my aunt Liz and her home on 20 Date Street. The house was a little mysterious because I would look up the long stairway to the second floor and wonder where do all the people sleep? My aunt Liz was my father's oldest sister. She was nine years older than dad. She would have eight children, five of whom would serve during World War II. To her credit she would have thirty-four grandchildren. I would have twenty-five first cousins with Helen McDonnell Buchheit the oldest and me the youngest. These numbers will be important as I get back to Sunday mornings at Aunt Liz's.

VISITORS TO MY STREET

Aunt Liz and Uncle Barney in front of 20 Date St. Mickey Buchheit going in the door. Ann (McDonnell) Giblin off to the right

The house was a modest dwelling with only a kitchen and pantry, dining room and living room and hallway on the first floor. A closed in porch out front would add space in the warmer weather. One bath and two bedrooms on the second with three more rooms in the attic. There was a two-car garage in the back, but I never remembered a car being in it. My uncle Barney would die in 1951 so he may have had one. I was named after him as my dad truly loved his brother-in-law.

Uncle Barney during Prohibition owned what is now Curley's Restaurant at Ridge and Electric Avenue. My dad would make wooden boxes for Uncle Barney, who would send the boxes empty to Toronto where they would be filled with liquor and marked "return to sender." My cousin Bernard McDonnel would verify that story for me. My dad's contribution to "bootlegging."

My grandparents were evicted from their Bethlehem Steel

company housing sometime in the twenty's. They then moved in with my aunt Liz who was already married with a family. After moving a couple of times, the family ended up on Date Street. Each of the non-married McCann brothers would live at 20 Date until they married and moved out. Thus, two families would be there with uncles and nieces and nephews living cheek to jowl. My dad would be the last to move out in 1937 when he and mom got married. My Uncle Tom, a confirmed bachelor, would never move out. He died in 1964. He lived a quiet life doting on his grand nieces and nephews, the Giblin family, my first cousin Ann's children, all seven of them, who would grow up at 20 Date Street. He was a steelworker. Every day as he would come home, he would somehow find time to buy treats or toys for those children. He was sweet hearted and kind. Never a bad word did he say. He pressed many a small coin into my hand without my dad knowing. I guess I too was part of his child spoiling operation.

In the early part of the 20th Century Uncle Tom was part of the Expeditionary Force under General Pershing that went into Mexico chasing Poncho Villa. Towards the end of his life, he started to tell the older nephews about his adventures. One I recall vividly was about how he saw Mexicans hanged on telephone poles going down a road for a great distance.

Uncle Tom also served under Pershing in France during World War I; there were stories told of surviving mustard gas attacks. That would put two brothers serving in World War 1, as his brother Joe was in the Navy for that war. He also told me that during his time in the Southwest chasing Pancho Villa's bandits, the rattlesnakes the US Cavalry troopers would catch and cook over a campfire, tasted much better than the canned Army rations given to his Cavalry outfit.

Back to Sunday mornings at Aunt Liz's. Sunday was mass

VISITORS TO MY STREET

day for the McCann-McDonnell clan. There was no Saturday vigil mass back then. Also, you could not eat or drink anything before going to communion at mass. Not everybody went to the same mass. At the Our Lady of Victory Basilica Sunday masses were at 6AM, 7AM, 8AM, 9AM, 10:30AM, the High Mass, and 12 noon. Aunt Liz would have breakfast ready for whoever came over after whatever mass. The 9AM mass was for school children so we always went to her house around 10:15. All the other cousins would show up at the same time. That meant I would have the Kane's, Buchheit's, and McDonnell's to play with after a quick breakfast. You were not allowed to stay long in the kitchen because another crew would arrive an hour later. My place at the kitchen table was always against the wall as there was no seat, only the steam radiator perfectly situated for a seat. It did get a little warm in the winter, but I did not care. Sitting there I would watch my cousin Gene who was in or just out of high school in the late forties, early fifties. He always seemed larger than life to me. There was always traffic going from the kitchen to the dining room and always someone going to the single bathroom. It was a babel of conversation and laughter. I was always in awe of my aunt how she flawlessly kept cooking and feeding everyone. This was not bowls of cereal. Eggs and bacon were continually cooking on the stove. Uncle Tom would often be the one doing the dishes and there were many of them to do. Most people stayed in the kitchen even if they had to stand, except us kids. We would be outside in a flash.

There was a chicken coop on the property behind my aunt's place. That would be the first place Bobby and I would go. For city kids chickens were somewhat exotic and a constant delight. These were the days when many of the twenty-five first cousins would get to know one another. It created a closeness that would last the rest of our lives. Not all cousins came. My uncle John and Art never came or brought their children. Consequently, I never knew those cousins until I was into adulthood.

Uncle Tom would become a focal point of family unity as he got older. There would be large picnics at Chestnut Ridge Park to celebrate his birthday each July. Once again, the Sunday crew would get together and enjoy each other's company.

Fast forward to 1984. I was working for the New York State Nurses Association as a Labor Representative. Often, I would have business in Buffalo, and I would stay at my cousin Helen's. One night we were sitting around, and I was talking with her and her husband John when the topic of two younger cousins came up. To this day I never knew who they were, but Helen did. A boy and a girl started dating. When their respective parents found out they were told that cousin dating was not allowed. Helen and I started talking about the Sunday breakfasts and the Uncle Tom picnics where all the cousins got together and, of course, knew each other. But now we were down to the next generation who did not grow up with that advantage. Using the Uncle Tom picnics as a model we declared that the last weekend in July would be a McCann/McDonnell reunion. We have had one each year but four since then. It is a much- anticipated event each year with cousins coming from the west coast, Colorado, New Hampshire, Florida, Pennsylvania, Massachusetts and elsewhere and, of course, the Buffalo area. I have not been to all of them, but the vast majority I was in attendance. They get to be more fun the older I get. Each year, I return with more photos of family members long gone to their reward. The young cousins marvel at how they resemble this uncle or that aunt.

There is a family resemblance passed down from generation to generation. A little of the Sunday mornings at Aunt Liz's house now happens at Firemen's Field in Hamburg NY each July.

Winter Afternoon Light

It is three in the afternoon on a cold, mid-January day as I sit by my computer and look out of my window facing to the west. I am immediately transported to my house on Colton Avenue which faced to the west. The late afternoon sunlight, even in winter, would come through our large front window into the living room. It somehow covered the walls in a soft glow that was comforting to a little boy intent on doing his homework before going out to play. Through the years this time of day, brief as it is, was always my favorite time. That soft glow of the afternoon sun brings me a personal contentment. This time would also be my most productive. I love reading in that undemanding light.

Bus Ride to Downtown Buffalo

Buying clothes for two young boys was a springtime odyssey for my mom and later for my dad and Fran and me. Some of my early memories were of long journeys from Lackawanna to downtown Buffalo. The trek would start by walking three blocks to the South Park Bus Stop. This was the end of the line for the NFT (Niagara Frontier Transit Line) heading south. The ride would take you through South Buffalo past Republic Steel and SOCONY Vacuum. The main point of interest for a little boy was the constant flame that was forever belching forth towards the sky from a high tower on the SOCONY property. This was an oil refinery right in the middle of the First Ward of Buffalo. Not something you see every day in a city. All these years, I have often wondered what SOCONY meant. It was while researching for this book that I found out it was not a word but an acronym for Standard Oil Company of New York. The plant was founded in 1880 as a source of fuel for booming plants in Lackawanna and Buffalo. They refined oil into Gasoline, Kerosene, and other fuels. Business would only grow as the industries it fed, grew through two world wars and the depression. Once Standard Oil bought the facility in 1892 it expanded at once. The Buffalo River along the refinery was dredged and straightened to allow lake tankers and barges to off load and discharge their cargo.

Sometime in the early fifties our Cub Scout Pack took a tour of the refinery. If you have never been to a refinery do not go without a gas mask. The facility smells something awful. Walking around the place I became sicker and sicker. The urge to throw up was overpowering. When they eventually took us into the control room, I did not want to leave the place. There was no smell in there. Somehow, I soldiered on and was happy to leave vowing never to return.

As SOCONY became Exxon and Exxon merged with Mobil, the refinery continued to run, focusing increasingly on distributing its goods via subterranean pipeline, rail, and truck, as its waterfront access was growing increasingly hazardous due to pollution. Following a series of river fires in the late 1960's, environmental concerns focused on the many

VISITORS TO MY STREET

factories, mills and, refineries operating along the Buffalo River, and for ExxonMobil the writing was on the wall.

Here is a side piece of information. Exxon was Esso for years and still is in South America and most, if not all, of Europe. Sometime in the early seventies or late sixties Esso starting marketing their products in Japan. The company executives were baffled by the low sales numbers until one bright MBA at Esso discovered the problem. You see that "Esso," in Japanese means "asshole." The name was quickly changed to Exxon both in Japan and the USA. All took place before large corporations paid any attention to foreign customs and language.

Continuing our bus journey to downtown the route would go through the First Ward past an industrial zone where one could see the Trico Building Number One. Trico, the maker of car windshield blades started operation in Buffalo in 1917 and kept their headquarters in Buffalo until the eighties. They had three factories at one time employing over five thousand workers. By the time it closed in the eighties they were down to 216 workers. The plant moved to the Tex-Mex border another casualty to the globalization of industry.

Buffalo is now playing at being a Phoenix. Out of the ash of empty buildings is coming new life. The Trico Building is being renovated to the tune of $80 million for a mixed-use development of apartments, hotel, medical facilities, and parking garage.

The next visual landmark, at the end of South Park Avenue as it turned right and became Main Street, was the Erie Lackawanna Railroad Terminal. I would look for trains and even sometimes catch a glimpse of a Great Lakes Cruise Ship that would be docked alongside the terminal. Just after the war my mom would take us to Corning NY, her hometown via the Erie Railroad. Her dad, my grandfather Thomas Moran, was a break man on the Erie RR. He died, as we mentioned earlier, in a railroad accident. Mom had free tickets on the Erie Railroad. I know we used this terminal before 1948 when we bought a car and no longer took the train to Corning.

My attention always turned to the other side of the street from the Terminal, the east side because there was an old ratty looking hotel called the Seaman's Home. Dad would just say that area is called "Skid Row." You would always see men sleeping along the front of the building. It was the Seaman's Home Association, founded to allow the vast number of the Lake freighter's crews to have a cheap place to stay during the winter months when they were ashore. As shipping gradually declined it become more of a home for derelicts and down and outs. In the end it was a sad symbol of a vestige of a former robust port city.

Traveling north on Main, I would next look to my left to view the "Aud." Officially known as Memorial Auditorium, a sports complex built in 1940 that would become a second home for me. I have already mentioned the college games my dad and I would go to. In addition, I watched wrestling on TV from the Aud every Friday night. Gorgeous George, the Masked Marvel, Ilio Dipaulo, a local favorite, Yukon Eric, Sky High Lee, Hans Schmidt, The Gallagher Brothers (bad guys), and Fritz Von Eric were all names known to Buffalo wrestling fans. Rumor had it that the Masked Marvel was, in fact, a local Catholic priest, Monsignor Franklin M. Kelliher. At one point Fr. Kelliher oversaw Father Baker's Working Boys Home in Buffalo.

Along with college basketball and wrestling, the Aud would host the Buffalo Bisons of the AHL, the Sabres of the NHL, the Braves of the NBA, high school basketball tournaments and even an annual Cotillion which I attended in 1960.

My dad still had a little of the joker in him. On our way to the Aud on Saturday nights he would ask if I had the tickets, while feigning looking for them. I, of course did not have the tickets. One night he played the same routine but this time neither he nor I had the tickets. He forgot them on the kitchen table. Having to turn around and drive all the way home had a sobering effect. He never asked if I had the tickets again.

All the different levels of the Aud were color coded. On the floor they were brown. Next level was the cushioned seats all colored red. The next level was blue with the highest level were all gray. How can one forget the gray seats in the upper levels of the Aud where you could get a nosebleed? Most nights our tickets were for somewhere in the gray heaven. That would not stop dad from sitting in the Reds with the cushion seats. Invariably, the rightful occupants would come along, and we would move a little higher, most times eventually to our designated seats. The memories of being with my dad on these Saturday nights are very dear to me. The Aud was and always will be one of my favorite places in Buffalo. I was totally bummed when I heard it was to be torn down in 1996.

When they eventually tore the Aud down authorities would discover that it sat on the original terminus of the Erie Canal. Today it is, as part of the Buffalo continuing Phoenix story, called Canalside, with a contingent of retired naval ships, including a submarine, restaurants, skating rinks, and veteran memorials, and a beautiful walkway along the lake.

Still on the bus, I remember one time when I was very young getting off a Trolley Car. These rail dependent vehicles would traverse all over downtown and into the suburbs, even to Lackawanna. They disappeared completely in 1950. It would take years before the tracks were all removed. I quietly chuckled to myself when I returned to Buffalo after the advent of the light rail system. The tracks of most of the light rail were very close to where the trolley tracks had been, at least on Main Street. It would be a repeat of history as the light rail helped destroy downtown Buffalo.

We would get off the bus along Main Street, usually somewhere near Kleinhans Men's Store. That would be our first shopping stop. It seems, in my memory, we always walked to the basement. That would disappoint this little boy because I then missed the elevator ride with the attendant and all.

The walk up Main Street would take us past Lafayette Square, with its statue of Lafayette, the Lafayette Movie Theater, the Lafayette Hotel, and the Electric Building. In later years, the new Buffalo and Erie County Public library would anchor the eastern end of the square.

In the forties and fifties downtown was a magical place. Here is where we went for first run movies or department store shopping. The theaters were the Paramount, The Lafayette, The Century, and Shea's Buffalo. The movies were continuous so if you came in on the middle you stayed until it reached the middle of the next showing. There was no clearing the theater at the end of the movie as they do today. Only when the prices started to go up to $5 did they start having showings at a particular time that your ticket was good for.

There were two live theater venues downtown. The Erlanger across from the Statler Hotel and the Studio Art Theater. My brother Fran remembered going to the Erlanger to see Kismet which must have been just before it closed in 1956. The theater sat 1,500 patrons. It was built primarily for the Statler Hotel as there was a tunnel from the Statler under Delaware Avenue into the Erlanger. Well known performers of that time appeared in productions at the Erlanger, including Basil Rathbone, Buffalo's own Katharine Cornell, Helen Hayes, Lilian Gish, Barry Fitzgerald, Orson Welles, Tallulah Bankhead, Beatrice Lillie, George M. Cohan, Ed Wynn, Alfred Lunt and Lynn Fontanne, Cecil Hardwicke, Gloria Swanson, Ethel Waters, Katherine Hepburn, and all the Barrymores, Paul Roberson, Maurice Evans, Judith Anderson, and Jose Ferrer.

I saw the *Fantastics* at the Studio Art in the sixties. It was wonderful theater in the round with an intimate feel to it. That play would remain a favorite of mine.

Speaking of live theater, one of the bands to play in Buffalo was Spike Jones and the City Slickers. He had a nationally broadcasted Radio Show every week. The music was satirical adaptations of popular and classical music. Sometime in the late forties my mom and dad took my brother and me to see him perform. My brother thinks we saw him at Shea's Buffalo, but I still think it was at the Lafayette. I remember they played "McNamara's Band." It was a favorite of mine, so I sang along. This was the last time I can remember my mom going out with us to any theater. That was the only concert I ever went to until I was old enough to go to Kleinhans Music Hall.

At Kleinhans Music Hall in the summers during the sixties they would have Pop Concerts with the Buffalo Philharmonic playing and with dancing after the concert. It was a classy evening. I will return to Kleinhans Music Hall when I discuss my piano lessons and the dreaded recitals.

I apologize, I digress again. We were on our way to buy clothes at Hengerer's. One trip I must mention was a trip to Hengerer's Department Store to buy new suits for Fran and me. Hengerer's was the high-end department store in Buffalo.

It was erected in 1889 and remodeled in the mid-sixties. It had seven floors with a mezzanine and a basement. You could buy anything and get your hair done and afterwards have lunch. The uniformed elevator girls took you from floor to floor. You could buy everything from furniture to appliances. We bought clothes once we were of high school age.

The store was interesting, but my story is about a salesman in the Men's Department. Dad would often take us to Hengerer's when we needed a suit or winter coat. There was an older fellow working in the Men's Department who would always greet us by name. He was on old-fashion salesperson in that he remembered his customers and he had the knack of knowing exactly the type and design that would please. My memory is that he would choose the suits for us to try on and invariably he would be spot on with the size and everything. I particularly remember buying a winter dress coat. I was in seventh grade and had stopped growing by that time. I would still be wearing that coat while in the Army twenty years later. Dad always said buy well-made clothes and they will last a long time. He was right as always. Never knew the guy's name but I never forgot him.

There were so many large department stores or just clothing stores. There were the following: Adam, Meldrum, and Anderson's (AM&A's), Kobackers, Bergers, Hens and Kelly's, Kleinhans Men Store, in addition to Hengerer's. More importantly there were no shopping malls or plazas that had outlets for these stores. If you wanted to go to them, you had to come downtown. In many ways the downtown stores killed themselves by giving the suburbs no reason to come downtown to shop in their stores.

One thing that has been abandoned in most American cities is the street sweeper. They would be a common sight in downtown Buffalo. A single man would push a large metal drum with two wheels that were larger than the drum. Attached would be a bracket for a shovel and a broom. The gutters would be swept often making sure the downtown area always looked fresh and clean of trash. Even in Lackawanna we had street sweepers. They could be seen going up and down the streets, even on Colton. There were two other machines that cleaned the streets. One was a gutter sweeper that scooped up debris and sprayed water to clean up to the curb. The second one was a water tank that sprayed water out the back covering the whole street. It kept the dust down in summer.

Any trip downtown would include a wonderful visit to Laube's Cafeteria at the corner of Pearl and Eagle. It first opened to the public in 1922 and would be a mainstay in Buffalo until 1968 claiming at one point to serve three thousand customers each day.

This place would be where I ate every Friday night until 1963. We may have gone after that, but I just do not remember. I say 1963 because that is where I ate the day John F. Kennedy was assassinated. My plan that day was to meet my dad at Laube's after I had taken the bus from Niagara Falls where I was attending Niagara University. From there dad would drive me home for the weekend.

I got out of my 11am Russian History class in St. Vincent's Hall about noon that fateful day. The first thing I noticed was small groups of students surrounding anyone with a transistor radio. Each group was sharing the news that the President was shot. My planned schedule was to take the first bus from the campus to downtown Niagara Falls where I would catch the Grand Island Bus to downtown Buffalo. I jumped on the bus without any further details of what happened. The people on the bus were all subdued keeping their thoughts to themselves. Some, I assume were praying. As we approached the Bus Terminal in Niagara Falls, we all knew the President was dead, as the loudspeakers at the terminal were playing the National Anthem.

The ride to Buffalo was as silent as a tomb. Everyone was in shock and did not want to talk. My thoughts were going all over the place. Was this going to mean war? Who did it? Why? Once in Buffalo, it was a long walk from the Greyhound Terminal, which was on Main Street north of Shea's Buffalo to Laube's cafeteria.

There was a news stand outside of Laube's and the guy was hawking papers by saying that the president was dead. The headline was three inches high on a very early edition of the Buffalo Evening News.

Laube's had the best Baked Halibut I have ever eaten anywhere. Mom and dad and then just dad would take us there every Friday until that November 22, 1963. It closed in 1968. On weekend nights there would be a line outside the building, stretching for a hundred to two hundred feet. Once you got into the cafeteria you stayed in line for another sixty feet or so until you hit the serving line. First came the salads and appetizers, then the vegetables followed by the meats and fish. I always got the same thing, mashed potatoes with gravy, cooked carrots, Halibut, and chocolate pudding and chocolate milk. The cashier was at the end of the serving line. Right next to her was a wonder of efficiency, a dumb waiter. As the staff cleared the tables and put all dishes on the same trays used by the patrons, they would load the trays on the dumb waiter that took everything to the basement where they were washed.

Finding a table was always a problem. There was an

VISITORS TO MY STREET

upstairs where we ended up. My first memory of dinning at Laube's was the problem of the bathrooms. Mom usually took me with her and as a precocious three- and four-year old I knew I should be with dad.

If I may divert for one other eatery important to us in downtown Buffalo. The owners of Laube's Cafeteria also had a high-end restaurant called Laube's Old Spain. It was located just north of Shea's Buffalo Theater. As you entered the restaurant you were teleported to Spain and inside a Spanish courtyard with stucco walls and curving archways. The wooden chairs with red cushions and backing contrasted with the ultra-white tablecloths making it appear you were in the old world of Spain. There was a mezzanine section with tables secluded under the curved archways. The menu included offerings of seafood, Spanish dishes including Paella. We would eat there on special occasions but not often after my mom died.

The kid's menu, at least in the late forties was interesting for younger people as all the meals had names taken from Disney's Pinocchio. For instance, Figaro was a Liver Dish for $.35, Pinocchio was a turkey dinner for $.45, Blue Fairy was scrambled eggs and bacon or a vegetable dish for $.25, Jiminy Cricket was a Lamb dish for $.45 and Lampwick was a Fish dinner for $.35. All meals came with a drink and dessert. One does not forget such offerings.

Back to the Cafeteria. After dinner we would walk towards the bus stop to return to Lackawanna. The bus stop was very close to a Dixie Hat Shop at Main and Court Streets. Mom would always stop to try on hats. She was very style conscience and had an array of hats. Of course, as a schoolteacher she had to dress up every workday.

The return trip had me watching for all the same sights

and sounds I saw on the inward trip. Buffalo had so many interesting places for a young boy to explore even from a seat on a NFT Bus.

In later years, while driving to downtown we would take the Lake Road (Furman Blvd) and must pass the area where the Tugboats docked. I always marveled at these small boats being able to push the large lake freighters around. Also docked with the Tugboats was the Fireboat. Sometimes you would see the spray shooting skyward when they were testing the equipment. That was a thrill for a small boy.

Outdoor Market at Clinton and Bailey

Many a Saturday morning dad would take us down McKinley Parkway to Clinton and Bailey where there was a very large outdoor market. They did not call it a Farmer's Market, but that was what it was. There were all sorts of vegetables and fruits being sold. It was such fun to walk up and down the rows looking at all the goods.

There was also a wholesale market next to the outdoor market. It was here that dad would buy bananas by the stalk, and grapefruit by the case. We could never eat all the bananas before they ripened so dad would always make a trip to our relatives, especially the Giblins and he would share the bounty. The grapefruit we kept for ourselves as that was a breakfast regular. I enjoyed going into the cooler rooms where the bananas were stored on big hooks. I have never experienced such a place since.

One year in December dad and I were at the market searching for the perfect Christmas tree. There were vendors selling pre-cut trees. Dad and I were going from place to place until one vendor came over to dad and asked, "You are Mr. McCann, aren't you?" Dad said "yes," and the guy gave his name and then dad remembered him. He was a former student of dads from years ago.

The man (I forget his name) went on to tell a story about he was a student in dad's "Shop Class." After graduating from high school, he took up carpentry, a profession he was inspired to start because of dad's "Shop Class." He said he made out quite well in that field and was able to buy a tree farm, thus selling the trees that day. He went on to say that if it were not for my dad, he never would have followed that path.

Then he asked what kind of tree we were looking for. We said a Blue Spruce about seven feet high. He showed us the most perfect tree I had ever seen. He would take no money. In fact, he insisted on delivering the tree to our house. He would do the same thing for the next five years, never taking a cent. Each year he and dad would enjoy a beer together and reminisce about the high school years. Dad was very pleased, and I was so very proud of my father.

Piano Lessons

One of my mother's prize possessions was an upright piano that graced our front hall room. It shared that space with the family desk and the only phone. Mom was determined that both Fran and I should learn how to play the piano. Mrs. Guarino, next door, would have the same ambition for Ross and Mary. Somehow David got out of that scheme.

Fran and I started lessons at the same time, right after the piano arrived at our home. Our teacher would be a local neighbor, Mrs. Dietrich. She lived with her adult son on Maple Grove near South Park Ave. Once a week we would walk the few blocks to her house and wait until whoever was before us to finish. Fran would go first so I had to wait some more for my turn. The lesson was forty-five minutes. Mrs. Dietrich was an older woman with tons of patience, especially with Fran. I remember the day when her patience must have run out. She called my mom and begged her to have Fran stop taking lessons. Musically inclined or interested he was not. I, on the other hand, while not being very good at it, was at least interested. I would struggle down to Maple Grove once a week for eight more years.

My music was always from the simplified music sheets. The favorite piece for me was, *Three Coins in a Fountain*. I also played all the Christmas tunes. The first Christmas Fran and I started playing, my mom would have us do a family Christmas caroling with us playing the piano. It only happened once and that was Christmas in 1949.

Practicing was hard for me. Life was so busy with friends and sports taking all my time. But I tried. She would always ask before each lesson began if I had practiced since last week.

The scary part of taking music lessons was the dreaded annual recital. It was always held at either, Mount Mercy Academy, Kleinhans Music Hall, or a fancy house in Buffalo the whereabouts I have long forgotten. For weeks prior to the recital, I would work on that one single piece, which I had to play perfectly for the recital. The night of the recital I was always scared. The whole family would attend, with Fran being happiest of all since he did not have to suffer what I did. All the other families of the other students would also attend.

Somehow, I got through each year's recital, but I hated them just the same.

When I graduated from elementary school, I decided that I had enough. Sports was taking over a larger part of my life, so something had to give, and it was piano lessons. I have regretted that decision ever since. I really loved to play and would enjoy tinkering with the piano whenever I got the chance.

Once I became a parent, I could not wait to buy a piano and inflict piano lessons on my daughters. They would be so much better at it than I ever dreamed of, but that is another story.

Thank you, Mrs. Dietrich.

Corning New York

My fondest memories were not all in Lackawanna or Buffalo, but in Corning New York. My mom was born in Corning in September of 1910. It was a summer routine to spend a week or two in Corning, first going by train and then by car after 1948. The car ride was not my favorite. Too often, I would get car sick in the back seat. After two or three episodes of that they bought a boaster seat with a steering wheel attached so I could sit in the front seat and pretend I was driving. My parents were nothing but practical.

The visit to Corning included seeing my Uncle Francis or Fee, as everyone called him. He and my aunt Peg were my Godparents. Uncle Fee was the manager of a local bank. They had two daughters my cousins Mary Catherine and Margaret or Meg as we called her. We did not stay with them, instead opting to stay with my mom's Godparents Joe Underiner and

Kate Maxner. They were known to me as Uncle Joe and Aunt Kate. They were brother and sister. Kate was a widow. Their house was a throwback to another century. The "ice box" was just that. A wooden contraption with blocks of ice to keep it cold. The stove was a wood cook stove. Doilies were everywhere on chairs and tables. They had a closed-in front porch that I loved to play on. Even in the bedrooms it was a throwback in time with a chamber pot under every bed.

In their backyard Joe had a garden with vegetables and fruit. My first picking of blackberries took place in that yard. I have been an avid picker of berries ever since.

Behind my mother's childhood home in Corning was an honest to goodness, Castle with turrets and all. It was used as an armory. It has long since disappeared.

The famous Corning Glass Center had not yet been built in the 1940's. Instead, there was a small circular building in the middle of the street adjacent to the Baron Steuben Hotel. Inside was a small gift shop and the mold for the Mount Palomar Telescope. That little shop always had things to interest a little boy. I sometimes would get a Kaleidoscope that would give me hours of entertainment.

I do not remember when, but the Corning Glass Ware store opened in Corning. Fran and I were mystified by its electronically operated front door. It was a first of its kind for us. Just walk up to the door and it automatically open. For two little kids from Lackawanna, that wonder would presage so many other innovations to come.

Joe would take Fran and me for walks to cool spots. At the end of his street which I may add was on the side of a steep hill, was a waterway called Monkey Run Creek. It had been a major problem for Corning residents from years of flooding. Sometime in the late forties or early fifties the city or more probably the Corps of Engineers turned it into one long culvert to flow into the Chemung River which ran through the middle of Corning.

Corning was like a trip back to an older time. We would play along the banks of Monkey Run. One of my biggest thrills was to visit Harris Hill near Elmira. This was a Glider Airport on the side of a large hill. The Gliders would be connected to a regular plane and towed off the side of the hill. Dad and Uncle Joe would take us up to watch. My whole life until now I have wanted to fly in a Glider. Sometime back in the early seventies I took my family (minus Brig who was not born yet) to Harris Hill. When we saw the price of the Glider ride my wife and I decided that we could only afford one of us to go. She won the coin flip. Someday I will make it.

Something else about the trips to Corning was the obligatory visit to Dad's best friend's sister who was a long-term patient at St. Joseph's Hospital in Elmira. She was a nun in the order of the Sisters of St. Francis. I do not know all the particulars, but the main illness was, so we were told, Leukemia. I do not remember the number of years we went to see her, but it had to be about three or four. She was always in her bed but as she talked to you is seemed like she was a citizen of the world. She would speak of visiting places or knowing people all over the world. Her gift each time was to Fran, who was a serious stamp collector, a package of used stamps from foreign countries. Sister corresponded with people from every corner of the globe.

Little children are supposed to get bored when adults talk about anything. Somehow that was never the case with Sister Concepta. Her stories were always interesting to Fran and me. Our two plus hour stays went by quickly.

As I got older, we stopped going to Corning on a regular

basis. We somehow lost touch with Sr. Concepta. Dad also lost touch with her brother, the previously mentioned, Ed O'Hara. Sometime in the eighties I happened to be in Buffalo, and I saw an obituary for another sister of Ed O'Hara. I only knew her as Mrs. Russ, a neighbor of ours from Crescent Avenue and a fellow teacher with my mom. I knew her children, so I went to the Wake. While talking with one of her daughters, I found out that Sr. Concepta did not have Leukemia after all and that she left the Hospital in the late fifties and was stationed at a private Catholic School named Stella Niagara, located just north of Lewiston NY. That school just happened to be three miles north of Niagara University where, first Fran, then I matriculated from 1956 to 1965. I was devastated to know all those years we were so close to her yet so far and did not know it. She had lived well into the 1970's without further contact from us. SAD!

The other reason we loved going to Corning was the annual visit to Watkins Glen State Park. Long before it became a car racing mecca, Watkins Glen State Park provided visitors with a marvelous walkway to the top of the Glen with views of waterfalls and a fast-flowing stream. It always delighted Fran and me no matter how many times we visited.

The OLV Environs

Back in Lackawanna and the neighborhood. I remember playing in the field just south of OLV Academy. There were piles and piles of marble stones and pillars scattered about in the field right behind houses facing South Park Avenue between Crescent and Leo. My presumption was always that they were the left-over marble from the building of the Basilica. That made sense given its location. My guess is that there was value left in the pile. I would have loved to have taken a small piece, but alas, I never did. Now it is gone, removed sometime in the seventies.

Another place that I enjoyed near to home was the OLV Hospital snack bar. This was for people who were working or visiting at the Hospital. It was also a favorite of a certain little boy who loved chocolate milkshakes. Dad loved them too, so he was never averse to my suggestion to visit the snack bar. The milkshakes would be some of the best I have ever had or that could be just memory playing tricks.

Very Important People

Speaking of OLV Hospital, another of Father Baker's accomplishments, they had one ambulance and I can remember only one driver. His name was Bruce Dickinson, and he was also a "Father Baker Boy." Bruce could be seen day and night out in the ambulance. Off duty he would always be around the "Corner," the intersection of Ridge Road and South Park Avenue at the Southridge Restaurant. He was a gregarious person with an easy manner conducive to putting people at ease in times of stress brought on by health issues. He was one of many Father Baker Boys who stayed in Lackawanna and made lives for themselves and were contributors to the community.

Two such individuals, Leo Newton and Bill Fisher had great influence on my life as a teenager and on my life in general. Leo Newton was already a legendary basketball and baseball coach when I first played for him in the fifth grade. Leo was the high school and grade school coach at OLV Academy. His OLV High School basketball teams were perennial champions of the Catholic League. The big game each year in the forties and early fifties was the OLV versus Lackawanna. I remember attending games with my dad at Lackawanna High School. (OLV had no gym) The gym was packed with screaming fans from both schools. It was another early introduction for me as to how exciting basketball could be. I do not remember who won any game, I just knew I wanted to be involved in that excitement sometime. Names from then would be heroes for me as I got older, Steve Garvin and Eddie Ambrose for OLV and Mark Balen for Lackawanna. Mark would eventually go on to Niagara on scholarship but would tragically be involved in a bad automobile accident that would end his playing days. As a JV player at Baker-Victory, Mark would be my coach. His no nonsense, hard practicing, constant drills would instill in me a theory of basketball coaching that would extend out more than thirty years of my own coaching career. Oddly, enough Steve Garvin was the JV coach before Mark.

Back to Leo Newton. I remember my first try out for the elementary school basketball team. I was in sixth grade. Prior to that I played in the Lackawanna Recreation League on an OLV team. That was when the three second lane was only five feet wide, and the "key" really looked like a "keyhole." No three-point shots, no palming the ball as they all do now. Two handed set shots were the norm. Even high scoring Mark Balen used a two-hand shot that came from behind his head. It was something to watch.

That first practice was held at the McKinley Elementary School as OLV had no gym. We could practice there each Tuesday afternoon because OLV got out early so Catholic students in public school could have religious education at OLV. They were let out early from their schools. Thus, McKinley was available for us to practice. The only other practice site for us was St. Francis High School gym in Athol Springs, New York south of Lackawanna. It was and is a private Catholic Boys School.

The first drill I remember Leo having us do was the chest pass. He would be anal about passing and just how it was to be done. Same with dribbling and shooting. Leo was all fundamentals. His practices and the ones portrayed in "Hoosiers," the movie, were very similar. I was beyond myself when he told me I made the team. That would be the only year I was not a starter on any team thereafter. OLV had not lost a league championship in decades and would continue that tradition for many years

Leo's influence was not just basketball (I also played two years of baseball with him). He taught sportsmanship as if it was the bible. You shook hands with your opponent as if you really meant it. You helped opposing players off the ground if they fell. You were a gracious winner and a good loser (although that only happened once a year as we never lost league games and would lose only deep into the playoff for the diocesan championship.) What I admired most about Leo was his devotion to his job and God. We would pray before the games but not asking to win but that all would play well, and no one would be hurt. His kindness to all was manifest. A better role model none of us could have had until Bill Fisher came along.

At the beginning of seventh grade, we were told Leo would no longer be our coach. He had decided to become a Holy Cross Brother. I was devastated, as were all of us who had played for Leo. When it came time for basketball tryouts, we met Bill Fisher. He worked on the South Buffalo Railroad, which was the railroad for the huge Bethlehem Steel Plant in Lackawanna.

Bill was also dedicated to fundamentals, sportsmanship and being good people. He was, however, very funny. We all got nicknames. He would make playing for him seem like a walk in the park, but all the time you were learning and gaining skill in your sport. If we lost it was never our fault. He would just tell us that the opponents were better than us on that day. He never gave nor acknowledged excuses. He never questioned the referees or umpires. He was always a perfect gentleman, but with a great sense of humor. I molded much of my thirty plus years of coaching Cross Country, Boys and Girls basketball and baseball and softball on imitating Bill Fisher and Leo Newton. Of the hundreds of games, I coached I never received a technical foul or was never asked to leave the field. To do otherwise would have shamed me in front of those two men both now long deceased.

There were funny stories about both men. There was never a school bus at OLV. For us to get to games or practice first Leo and then Bill would use their own cars. Well, at least in basketball we always had ten players. Leo owned a four door 1948 Chevy. He had that thing right up to becoming a Brother. There would be three in the front seat, five or six in the back seat and as many as he could fit in the trunk. I remember one Saturday morning we were coming back from a practice at St. Francis. A police officer pulled Leo over for obvious reasons. (Of course, there was no seat belt law then.) The policeman asked what Leo thought he was doing. Leo went on with a long tale about Monsignor Maguire's car broke down at the last minute before taking the boys to the game (he upped the importance of the trip). That left him with only his car to transport the boys. At the mention of the Monsignor's name everything changed. The policeman admonished Leo to drive safely back to OLV.

Bill Fisher would do the same thing but would have a Studebaker Lark that was very compact shall we say. By the time Bill came along parents started helping a little bit.

My dad will always be the greatest influence on me as was my brother Fran. But those two coaches taught me, first how to play both games very well and then how to be a good sport. As time would have it, I would see coaches in town leagues, school leagues and even in the Army where I also coached and there were darn few that even came close to matching the wisdom of those two men. I was so lucky to have lived, at that time, in that city, at that school and to be under the influence of those two great men.

Leo would eventually leave the brotherhood and return to his beloved OLV, but long after I had graduated. He would coach my younger Giblin cousins. Too infrequently, I would return to OLV and practice with him and his team. By this time there was a nice new gym and no more transporting kids in the trunk of the car. Leo was older but it was so nice visiting and reminiscing with him.

As for Bill, we exchanged Christmas cards for years until his death. When I would be in Lackawanna, and I would go to mass at the Basilica, where Bill was always an usher. We would meet for coffee after mass. Those too few moments with the men who helped shape my life would be important reminders of what one person can mean to another. We are all shaped by things and people around us. I thank God those men were in the path of my life.

Going to School at OLV

OLV Academy would provide me with any number of wonderful teachers. From First grade with Sister Ellen and on to Sister Perpetua in second grade, they both gave me the first inkling that I loved to learn. But it was in Fourth Grade that I was inspired and motivated by a woman who helped direct my life. Her name was Miss Hoffmeir. To this day I was never aware of any first name. She was slightly older than my third-grade teacher, Miss Hagel, who, I was sure was right out of college and that we were her first class. Miss Hoffmeir was probably in her late twenties. She had a calm demeanor that had us kids being calm also. I am sure she took extra attention with me because of my mom dying the previous spring. But she was attentive to all her students, in the kindliest ways. Looking back, it is hard to recall just what made her special, but I know that she conveyed to us that learning was important and that she was there to help us achieve whatever we wanted to do.

I remember while in High School, I saw her working in a paper supply store as a clerk. I felt bad that she had to work after school. It was not right. She was the best teacher in our school and should be rewarded with a large salary so she would not have to work two jobs. I was incensed about that. Guess I did not know the reality of Catholic School teachers working for less than adequate wages.

She felt like a guardian angel looking out for each one of us. I remember her having a story time each day. Her voice would make the story come alive as if we were watching a movie. I hated to be promoted to the next grade. It saddens me that I could never share with her that I became a schoolteacher and that I remembered so much of what she taught about what it meant to be a great teacher.

The other nun who had such a great influence on me was Sister Mary Frances Borgia. She taught eighth grade, but I never had her. I did have a wonderful teacher for eighth grade, in Sister Catherine, who I adored. But Sister Borgia was a sports fan. She came to all our games and quietly cheered us on. Before each game she would call the whole team to her room and line us up along the chalk board. Then she would go over a list of things we had better have right. Was our uniform clean? Did we have clean white socks? Were we going to win?

Sister Borgia looked old, and she did not smile much, which gave her a serious look. But she loved us and wanted nothing but good things for each of us. The last time I saw her I was riding a bus from Albany, New York to Buffalo. I was in Law School at the time. As I walked down the aisle, I saw her sitting alone, still in the habit that she wore when I last saw her in eighth grade.

When I sat down next to her, she beamed for she recognized me at once. When I told her I was a law student she was beside herself with pride. The next six hours or so went by with each of us talking non-stop. The trip ended all too soon. That was the last time I saw her, but I would never forget her.

People of my age will tell horror stories of how nuns had beaten them in grammar school. But I can tell you that was not my experience. Each nun I had was a loving and kind person.

Maybe Sister Emmanuel (seventh grade) got a little excited sometimes, but I put that off to her age. One day she asked me if I would go with her to the Post Office after school. The Post office was located across from the public high school, and she said she was afraid of the public high school kids. I said to myself to myself, "you want me to protect you, you who could slash my hands with a ruler (she never did)." I was the tallest boy in the class which is why she asked me. The irony was lost on her.

Those eight years at OLV truly shaped my life. From sportsmanship in athletics, to a love of reading and to a love of learning that has lasted a lifetime. OLV was my guiding light. It is reassuring that the halls of this wonderful school still echo the steps of young people on a similar journey. It is also nice to know that these journeys have been going on for the last 120 years.

The School Playground

OLV was more than just a school to those who used its play yard. It was a safe place to play. Today's children would have a hard time understanding how a play yard could be such a wonderful place with no playground equipment. No swings, no wood chipped areas, just macadam surface with a six-foot fence around it and one gated (no lock) entrance. The south wall of the school made up the north side of the yard. The only equipment, per se, were two basketball backboards and hoops. We had to make our own lines for foul shots. The three second rule was not yet an issue.

The basketball court was used year-round. Someone would bring a shovel to remove enough snow to allow for a half-court game. It was a hub for local neighborhood basketball. All games were pick up type, with two captains (the bigger kids) picking team after an odd or even toss of the hands to see who went first. If enough players were around and waiting to play, they would form an appropriate size team and call winners. That gave them to right to play against whichever team, currently playing, won the game.

In the warmer weather two guys could make up a full baseball game and spend hours playing. We called it "fast pitch." All you needed was a halfway decent tennis ball, a bat, chalk, and knowledge of a big-league team. With the chalk you drew a strike zone box on the school building away from any windows. The box, once drawn was there for a long time. The bat was to hit the tennis ball. The ball was pitched from a spot approximating distance from the pitcher's mound. If the batter swung and missed, or if it hit the strike zone that was a strike. Outside the zone was a ball. A hit ball that was a grounder if caught was one out. A fly ball over the pitcher's head was a double. A fly ball that hit the fence was a triple. Anything on the ground going past the pitcher was a single. If you caught a fly ball with one hand in the air and a double play was possible it was a double play. A hit fly ball over the fence was a home run. All base runners were imaginary, as only two people were playing the game.

You needed to know about major league teams because each player picked a team and had to follow that team's starting lineup exactly because you had to hit left or right depending on how the major league player would hit.

You played nine innings and could easily play a doubleheader. I cannot guess at how many games I played over the years, but it was a lot. There was also a two-man team version with rules slightly altered. I highly recommend such a game to children. I became equally adept hitting from either side of the plate because of that experience.

Then there were all sorts of variations of softball. If you only had four people, then the "field" was reduced to right or left. Anything hit to other field were automatic outs. That taught me how to direct my swings to hit where I wanted the ball to go. Often, we had full nine people a side and always co-ed. One game I remember very well. The ages of the players could vary by five or six years. At one point I was on third base. I do not remember how I got there but there I stood. At bat, was my teammate, Evie Callsen, who was same age as my brother. She was a good hitter, so I was ready to run home when she hit it. Well, she hit it all right, a line shot right down the third baseline and directly at my temple. I went down like a sack of potatoes. I was momentarily out but not hurt. Just recently I reconnected with Evie, sixty-five years later. She remembered the incident very clearly because she was so worried, she had killed me.

There was no adult supervision, we did not need any.

I could not say there was no adult, there was one who played and taught us as he played. That was Mr. Albee who live directly across the street on South Park Ave. He had three children; his youngest Ray was in my brother's class. He had an older brother and an older sister. The older brother would die in a freak accident in Korea as I remember. Ray would become one of the greatest all-time scorers in the Catholic Basketball League. In pre three point shot days he averaged close to thirty points a game, earning him a scholarship to University of Detroit. He would have a fair playing teammate, Hall of Famer Dave DeBusschere, of the New York Knicks. I saw most every game Ray played in high school. I am sure his dad had much to do with his success.

Mr. Albee would always be ready for a game of twenty-one or horse or pig. His shot repertoire was amazing to us kids. He was the master of the trick shot, which made it hard to beat him in horse. With that said he would let us win on a consistent basis. Along the way, he would by example and overtly teach us about how to play effective basketball. I suppose I learned about moving without the ball from him. It was as if he was following the credo of Leo Newton and Bill Fisher. What also amazed me was that Mr. Albee never got tired. I cannot even guess how old he was at that time. He also supplied a basketball, which always seemed to be in short supply.

He was another of those special people living in my neighborhood who I was lucky enough to have interacted with. Thank you, Mr. Albee.

The school playground was also used as a holding pen for students during lunch time. The kids who stayed at school would eat and then go to the playground. It had no equipment just open space and two hoops. I would hurry back from home (two blocks away) so I could either get in a game of basketball or any of a myriad of games. That is where I learned to do double-dutch in jump rope. All eight grades would be in the yard by the time the bell rang. We would then quickly line up by grade and march into school. On inclement weather days I took my time coming back as no one was allowed out of the building and being stuck in the classroom was no fun.

Another spot we played different forms of baseball or softball, or kickball was a then vacant lot on the north side of Crescent and Victory. It was a small lot eventually filled with a single-family house. It was right next door to Bob Hartman's house. Because it was so small, we usually played kickball with a very soft ball so no damage would come to vehicles or houses in proximity. The bases could not have been more than fifteen feet apart. What fun we had there for hours. An additional bonus of using that lot was that it bordered the back yard of Mrs. Murphy. She had a wonderful grape vine growing on the fence facing our ballfield.

Sometimes we would partake of those delicious grapes. She never seemed to mind.

Victory Playground

While talking about play areas, my summer place to be was Victory Playground. This was a city-run facility just one block over and two blocks down. As I write this an old friend just sent a message to me on Facebook. His name is Ron Young, and he lived right next to Victory playground. Thinking of him recalled all the adventures and fun times that playground afforded me and all the children of our neighborhood. In the summer it would open at 9am and close at sunset. There would be a watcher as we called them. For years, the watcher was Ann Marie Shea, who was around my brother's age and lived just behind us on Victory. She would lay out a blanket and be available if anyone needed her. She knew everyone and was always friendly.

There were big swings with wooden seats that could crack your head open if you got hit and that happened at least sometimes each summer. We would have jumping contests off those swings. Each participant would pump themselves as high as they dared and then jump off. This kind of contest could use up a lot of time. But time was what we had. If you were smart you would bring something for lunch and thus be able to play all day until supper time. No one would dare miss supper.

There was also a flagpole and Ann Marie would raise the flag each day. Next to it was the sandbox, about ten by ten but seemed much larger and only shrunk as children got older.

VISITORS TO MY STREET

Near that was the push yourself merry-go-round that delighted children of all ages.

Up to a certain time there was a ball field with a backstop that stopped few balls because of the holes in the fencing. This is where I learned to play softball. In the mid-fifties each playground in the city had its own softball team. Now unfortunately, I must report that this team was only for boys. Girls just did not have those opportunities for formalized sports. Oddly, they were always welcome for the pick-up games. Speaking of female athletes I must mention, Helen Marie Kaney, as she was the best female athlete I ever knew as a child. She certainly was a better athlete than many of the boys. She would be chosen into a game ahead of some boys. I have not seen her since our childhood, but I did hear that she became a lawyer

The softball team would be a great adventure. We got to go to other playgrounds to assess our skills against other kids. Pat Malone, who was a little older and lived across the street from the playground would coach us sometimes. I was the catcher and Henry Wietchy was the pitcher. Henry was also the best hitter. Great fun and we all got along.

At night, we would switch to hardball and play under the lights at Lackawanna Stadium. This was a City Recreation League team representing OLV. The previously mentioned Bill Fisher would coach us. There were four teams each year in the league. There were two divisions for younger (up to fifth grade) and then older (up to eighth grade). I played one year in the younger and the rest in the older division. The four teams each stood for an area or ethnic group. Our team was OLV and had mostly Irish kids on the team. There was the Armstrong Athletic Club, playing out of the Friendship House, being the African American community. Playing against them was when people of different races could interact with each other. Sadly, Lackawanna was a segregated community. Not totally, as schools were integrated, but housing was not. All African Americans lived on the side of the city nearest the steel plant. There were New York Central Railroad tracks running through the middle of town and they effectively became the housing barrier. I enjoyed those games and made nice friends in the bargain. Only recently, I reconnected with one the best AAC players, Dickie Freeman. We played both baseball and basketball against each other. It was always a good game.

Another team was from Bethlehem Park, a small community within the city, right across the road from the steel plant. Originally built to house workers from the plant. By the time I was growing up Puerto Rican families occupied the Park. Thus, the team mirrored the population.

The last team was the Warsaw Athletic Club. Most, if not all players were of Polish descent. Lackawanna had a very large Polish community. Geographically that area would start one block to the west of Colton Ave. on Electric Avenue and would then run south towards Warsaw Avenue and west towards the Railroad tracks.

There was also a team from Ridgewood Village found on the east side of town. By the time I got involved playing they had disbanded. Ridgewood Village was originally built as temporary housing during World War Two. Gradually, the units became owned by the occupants. They still survive quite well today.

Street Dances

One of the most expected events around the playground each year was the Street Dances. Toward late August the Recreation Department of Lackawanna sponsored neighborhood street dances. Next to the Victory Playground, the street would be closed off enough to allow dancing. Music would come over a loudspeaker and everyone enjoyed the dance. I remember being too little to understand the allure of dancing but that would change around seventh grade. A warm summer night with music in the air made living in Lackawanna a little more romantic.

I would be remiss if I did not mention Ralph Galanti, the head of the Recreation Department. Ralph worked tirelessly for the sports programs in Lackawanna. He would always be around the games to make sure things went well. He is another of those Lackawanna men who contributed so much to my life. In later years when I was the City Attorney of Glens Falls, New York, Ralph would follow my career through his friendship with the Glens Falls Recreation director, Dan Reardon. Just being from Lackawanna always connected people. I now stay in touch with Ralph's son, Ralph Jr., through Facebook. He too has written about what a magical place Lackawanna was and still is.

The Drug Store

One of the things I remember about my dad was his love of treats. We would walk to Parson's Drug Store. They had the old fashion soda counter where you could get lunch or ice cream. I suppose they did breakfast, but I was never there for that. Dad loved to take Fran and me for a treat. I developed my love of Banana Splits at Parsons. That is what I usually ordered. Today such a pleasure would entail lots of money. Back then it was the simple fact of being with my dad and both enjoying what we ate.

Parson's always makes me think about the Legion of Decency. This was a squad of men from the Catholic Church who would routinely visit the magazine section at Parson's and other drug stores or any outlet that sold magazines. They would check to see if anything were being sold that was on a Prohibited List published by the Diocese. Hard to imagine today but back then being so close to the Basilica they had influence. Not sure what they made the store do if anything.

Caretaker of the Community

I suppose all communities have their own beloved doctor, their own "Dr. Kildare," if you would. Ours was Dr. Gene Sullivan. He was there at my birth, he gave me all my school physicals, he stitched me up when I put my hand through the front door, and he came to the house late at night when my grandmother was having a heart attack. It was not just that he did all those things but the way he did it. Always patient, always understanding with empathy to spare. His life was his patients. His office and home were across the street from the Basilica. I just cannot imagine him having much free time. His dad was a Father Baker Boy which just adds to the mystique around Dr. Gene. He was my mother's primary care doctor, although they did not use that term back then. I remember him coming to the house on more than one occasion. Again,

I and all of us in Lackawanna were lucky to have such a good man as our doctor and a visitor to our street.

Neighborhood Gathering

Going back to the late forties and very early fifties there was an event in our neighborhood, a visitor if you will. On Crescent Avenue, a few doors from South Park lived the City's Fire Chief, Chief Quinn. He was another of those beloved characters that Lackawanna had in abundance. Everyone knew Chief Quinn as they knew Police Chief Curtin, who was also much loved by the community.

Chief Quinn's back yard went from Crescent to Leo Street. It was long and narrow. In the fall it was the location of many a hard-fought touch football game. I was too young, but my brother played. Once a summer Chief Quinn would sponsor a neighborhood picnic in his backyard. There were hot dogs and hamburgers and corn on the cob. The corn, I remember was especially good as they cooked it in sand. There was a big black cooker filled with sand and a fire underneath. I do not know if Chief Quinn paid for all that or not, but it was an exciting event. There was more than one, but I remember it being just one year.

I knew most families on Colton were Catholic. There may have been others but the only family that was not Catholic that I knew was the Hendra Family who lived on the corner of Crescent and Colton. They had what I thought at the time was a big yard. There were three boys, Fred, my age, and Jim and Terry, who were younger. For some reason they did not come onto the street to play with the myriad of other kids our age. They always stayed in the yard. I thought that strange, but I never dwelt on it. I liked the Hendras. Their mother was always kind and pleasant, even inviting me for lunch sometimes. Their grandfather lived with them, and I am pretty sure he was a sexton or some other type of official at the Bethel Protestant Church on Ridge Road. He would often be working around the church.

The boys and I would play in their yard games of baseball and football, and about every other game we could think of. There was no father as far as I could tell. My mom would talk with Mrs. Hendra sometimes on her way home from school. Aside from that there was very little interaction with other neighbors and the Hendras. The Callsen's across the street from them would sometimes play in the yard. Looking back, I must believe that their religious affiliation had something to do with that separation. It was too bad, as they were a very nice and kind family.

Mom's Best Friend

I could not write about my early life without mentioning a dear friend of my mother's, Betty Nash Gormley. They were two peas in a pod. Both taught high school at Lackawanna High and were about the same age. After mom died Dad thought it important that we continue the friendship. He somehow knew how important it would be to Betty. I am sure it was important to him to have us be friends with mom's best friend. Betty would pass away May 25, 2004, and her funeral would be at Holy Family Church described below.

Betty was the niece of Monsignor John J. Nash, the founder and long-time pastor of Holy Family Parish on South Park Ave., in South Buffalo. It was a huge church built in 1902. Fr. Nash, as we called him was the pastor for 53 years until his death in 1953.

My mom and Betty were frequent visitors to each other's homes. Betty lived in a big mansion on McKinley Parkway in South Buffalo right on the west side of McClellan Circle. It had large pillars gracing the front porch. When my children were still young, we would stay with Betty in that big old house. The best feature for me was a huge grandfather clock that chimed each quarter hour with special chimes for the half hour and the hour. So many rooms and even in the eighties the rooms were as I remembered from the fifties. Each visit was a trip back in time

Betty loved seeing my children, as they were for her, a connection to her best friend, my mother. Much of what I remember about my mom was from listening to Betty tell stories about her.

Betty's family was very religious. Her uncle obviously, but also her mother. I remember when her dad died, her mom instead of embracing widowhood, joined the Carmelite Sisters in Buffalo. The convent was located on Carmel Drive, just off Hertel Avenue. That convent is the site of the Shrine of the Little Flower of Jesus. I remember our family all going to a special service honoring St. Theresa. The then Bishop, and later Cardinal John O'Hara presided. There were dozens of priests and nuns. The cloistered nuns were behind a screen off to the side of the main altar. During the ceremony they passed out small flowers to each person. My mom kept them pressed in a book which I found years after she died. The flower is still flattened by years of pressure from the closed book.

Betty's mom was not one of the cloistered nuns. She was the out-front person who would greet guests and answer questions. There was sort of a Lazy Susan built into the wall where you could place things. As you turned the device it would open on the other side of the wall and the cloistered nuns could retrieve it. It was something that intrigued a small boy.

The cloistered nuns would not speak except for prayers and song and special occasions. They had no news of the outside world except for Catholic literature. Once a month they could have visits from their families. They were allowed to correspond with their families by letter. The purpose of the cloister was to allow the nuns to dedicate their lives to prayer and contemplation. There were two such convents in Buffalo, the other being the Dominican Nuns of the Perpetual Rosary. As of 2012, both convents were still functioning.

Back to Betty's family, her daughter Mary would become a Sister of Mercy and would be assigned, at least for a while, at Mount Mercy High School in South Buffalo. It has been years since I had had any contact with Betty's children. I would stop occasionally at the old house on McClellan Circle and visit with her youngest son. But that was years ago. One week after writing this paragraph I would receive a phone call from a Sister Mary Ellen Twist who was calling to thank me for a donation I made to OLV Academy. I thanked her and just as I was hanging up, I realized what she said that her name was Twist. This is an old Lackawanna name with which I was familiar. Later that day I called her back. It turns out she was a Twist from Lackawanna and that she was related to any number of my childhood friends. She was also a Mercy nun and knew Betty Gormley's daughter, Mary. In addition, she knew my dear friend from childhood Cecilia Cosgrove, who I had not seen in 58 years. Cecilia's dad taught with my mom and her brother Ed was a prominent lawyer in Buffalo when I was just starting out. He often gave me encouragement. The world of Lackawanna was small, indeed.

Betty would come one time to visit us in Glens Falls sometime in the early eighties. She would stay at Garnet Hill Lodge, in North River. Betty's letters were something to read. I wish I had saved them. Her English and phraseology were of another era. I marveled at how she could turn a phrase. No one talks or writes like that anymore and have not for one hundred years.

Why People Were So Close

There are close ties to many people living in Lackawanna. In 1940 there were only 24, 058 people living in Lackawanna and ten years later it was only 27,658. If you pare that down to the people who lived in the OLV parish the number becomes closer to 2,000. You add to that the large families who lived in Lackawanna since its growth with the building of the Steel Plant. A significant percentage of the families were involved with the migration from Scranton PA in the early 1900's such as the McCann's. That means, in Lackawanna that residents had close ties even before arriving in Lackawanna.

The other thing that kept my friends and relatives together was their faith. The Catholic Church had built an infrastructure, as it were, for Catholic Society. There were groups for Catholic lawyers, doctors, and teachers. You could go to all Catholic Schools, and Universities. Your social arrangements could be with the Knights of Columbus and Catholic Daughters Society. There was church-sponsored Boy Scouts and Cub Scouts. I do not remember there being any Girl Scout Troop. Girls did not have the opportunities open to boys.

My point being that the Catholic Church had created a parallel society where Catholics could exist untainted by the wider world. This would shrink the society in Lackawanna that I was part of well into my late teens. As I previously said, the Hendras were the only Protestants that I knew. I would not meet a person of the Jewish faith until I attended New York's Boys State. His name was Artie Heyman, from New York City. I guess you could say I lived a sheltered life up until then. Most of my playmates went to the same school and church.

The Bat

Memories often come from photographs or letters or just things. One thing I have kept all these years is a softball bat. My dad made this bat in his Shop classroom. For years I used that bat for softball or fast pitch. Today it is combined as a memory of my father and my mother. Dad obviously for making it for me and for my mom I must add another story. It was sometime in the late forties. My mom and dad took Fran and me to Old Forge NY. Mom while at Plattsburgh State Normal had worked there for a family whose name has escaped me. They owned an Inn, in Big Moose, NY just outside of Old Forge. I have tried to find that Lodge in the last few years, but it burned down. I remember one day while sitting in their kitchen noticing a baseball bat next to the screen door. Being curious I picked it up and began swinging it around hitting imaginary home runs. The old cook came over to me and asked if I knew what that was, I had in my hands. I said, "a baseball bat." She said, "No, it is not." I was confused until she said it is a Bear Bat. I said, "What is a Bear Bat?" Her answer was to the effect that if a Bear came into the kitchen, she could beat it off with the Bear Bat. Since moving to the Adirondacks fifty years ago I have always had a Bear Bat by the back door, and it has always been the bat that Dad made for me so many years ago. It graces our door in the kitchen even now. So going out the door when I see that bat, I think of both my mom and dad and love just pours out of that beat up old bat. P.S. I have never chased a bear with it.

Crystal Beach

For people of a certain age in Western New York and southern Ontario, there was no more magical place than Crystal Beach. The decades before I was born it was a favorite spot for bathing, dancing, hearing big bands and, of course, the amusement park.

Located along the shore of Lake Erie, in Canada about a thirty-five-minute drive from the Peace Bridge, this was a summer destination for young and old alike. From Buffalo the best way to get there was by boat. There had been two large boats that would traverse the distance between Buffalo and Crystal Beach. They were the Americana and the Canadiana. By the time I became a passenger, the Canadiana, built in 1910, was the only one crossing Lake Erie to and from the park.

The Park had great rides such as the Magic Carpet, Tunnel of Love Boat, The Giant Coaster, the Fun House, the Laff in the Dark, Bumper Cars and of course, the Comet. In addition to the rides, there were arcades, the Dance Hall, picnic areas and a wonderful "crystal" beach.

To a little boy Crystal Beach was a "magic kingdom" before there was a Magic Kingdom. The first time I went to Crystal Beach was with my school. Annually, in the spring, the nuns would start collecting ticket money from the students. I remember getting money from my dad, putting it into a brown envelope given to me by my teacher and then turning it in at school. We all loved the anticipation of that wondrous day. I do not know how they got busses, but we were at school early to board the busses. I can remember waiting in line to board the Canadiana, the only real boat I had ever been on, except for a rowboat. I watched as Buffalo would fade into the distance and then disappear as we rounded the Canadian shoreline. It was pure exhilaration as we peered over the railing and into the frothy lake. Then our attention was drawn to the shoreline as the long pier jutted out with the Comet looming overhead.

It felt like entering Ellis Island, being a foreign country and walking down this crowded pier. The line went so slow, and we were so excited to get into the park it was hard to be patient. To our left we could see the famous "Crystal" beach. It always looked so inviting with clean, bright sand.

At last, past Customs, we were in the park. The sisters had us group with buddies and off we would go. Each of the rides mentioned above would be a destination. Our tickets were clasped tightly in our hands as we decided which ride to go on first. My favorite, as a youngster, was the Fun House. The slanted room that you had to navigate back and forth around the metal railings was such an adventure. The rush of air that pushed the girl's skirts up was always funny and could be seen from the outside. Girls did a Marilyn Monroe pose, before even she made it famous in "Some Like it Hot."

The Magic Carpet ride was also a favorite. I do not remember what was inside, but the exit was down a long carpet-like conveyor belt into a soft-landing area.

I was too young to go on the Comet but did go on the Yellow Rollercoaster and that was scary enough. The day would seem to go on forever but eventually we had to return to the boat and head home to await another year to visit Crystal Beach.

The Canadiana would take its last cruise on Labor Day of 1956. This ended forty-six years of making the crossing of Lake Erie to and from Canada. A tragic brawl or riot, as they called it then, would be the straw that broke the camel's back. It was a mini race riot according to the newspapers. The boat ride was not making money for the owners for some time. Ticket prices were kept artificially low to attract customers. The purpose of the boat was to get passengers to and from Crystal Beach. To do that, the owners had to keep ticket prices artificially low. Thus, the boat owners were losing money. But after that incident where teenagers were injured and arrested, the boat ride to Crystal Beach was no more.

As a college student I went back twice. Once on a date and once with my college roommate Mike Fleming. Somehow it was not the same. My last time at Crystal beach was 1975 when my family and I went with my dear cousin Sue and her husband Pat Duggan. My Brigid was only six months old; Casey was five and Kelly seven. Somehow my girls did not have the same magical experience that I had at their ages. The Park by that time had become a little weary and tarnished.

Once the park closed the Comet was sold to the Great Escape Amusement Park in Lake George. At the time I lived about a quarter mile from that park. We could hear the screams of the riders from our house. I started riding the Comet every summer since then with my last ride in 2019 at age 75. The thrill was and is still there.

Riding a Bike

Back to Colton Avenue, I remember the day that I borrowed a friend's bike with training wheels. It had all sorts of cowboy gear on it. I would ride down Colton as fast as my little legs would carry me. My Roy Rogers six gun drawn and firing at all the bad guys. That was heady stuff for a five-year-old. How I wished for that bike. My wish never did come true.

Being a younger brother by five years makes taking over play equipment or even clothes a difficult job sometimes. I would get all of Fran's hand-me-downs, even sometimes wrapped and gifted at Christmas. One of my favorites was his dress winter coat. It was very modern, and I felt so old when wearing it. His "white bucks" were another matter. They did not fit for a few years and so were not very comfortable. But I wore them just to look like Fran.

The first bike I received was a hand-me-down twenty-six inch that belonged to Fran. The bike was just too big for me. Reaching the bike peddles was beyond the length of my legs. Our driveway between our house and O'Leary's was a playground for those who played alone. It would serve many functions over the years. Beautiful Tiger Lillies grew along O'Leary's side, as did the quiet, little, Lillies of the Valley. A small median divided the driveway with sparse patches of grass growing where the sunlight would sometimes land. An old, two-piece swinging gate would mark the half-way point to the garage.

The driveway cement went right up to the house. That allowed me to climb up onto our back porch and then climb down to mount that very large bike. I would push off from the porch and hope that I could steer along the side of the house heading for the street. Many, many times I would go off and fall. But as many times as I fell, I would get back up until that one day that I reached the end of the house. It took two years for me to reach that point. My knees attest to the all the falls. Eventually, I would be out on the street and the bike would be my mode of transportation within the city for years.

Lent and Easter Season

As I write this we have just gone through Lent and Easter Week. With everyone ordered to stay at home because of the Covid 19 pandemic, it did not feel much like Easter. In grade school Lent took on a very special quality. Mass was a daily occurrence with breakfast in school at our desks. Those little cereal boxes that you added milk to, became our breakfast staple. On First Fridays however, we were served sweet rolls in the cafeteria. A treat for me even to this day. My good wife will surprise me occasionally, with a dozen sweet rolls. Just the taste transports me back to the OLV cafeteria and those First Friday treats. I should mention who gave out those wonderful "sweet rolls." It was Mrs. Garvin. She was my cousin, Jimmy McDonnell's mother-in-law. His wife, Rose McDonnell was the oldest of nine Garvin children, who would be dear friends, from Theresa, a year older than me to Paul, a year younger and Mickey two years younger. Mrs. Garvin was also a friend of my mom's, so every time I came through the line, I got two sweet rolls instead of one. She would live a long life and I loved her very much.

Easter Week was really a whole week of religious services at OLV. Monday through Wednesday night, there was a service called Tenebrae. It was a traditional celebration. The word means "Shadow." The services were with the church lights out as a symbol of the darkness to come. There would be scripture readings and on Tuesday night a reading of the long gospel telling the story of Christ's sacrifice. At the conclusion of each service the candles would be extinguished and loud noises like thunder could be heard. As a young Altar Boy, I would serve each night of Tenebrae.

On Holy Thursday, the tradition was to visit seven churches. That was not a problem because of the plethora of churches in our immediate vicinity. The churches were mostly ethnically rooted. Just in Lackawanna were the following: Catholic Churches, St. Michael's (Polish), St. Barbara's (Polish), St. Anthony's (Italian), St. Hyacinth's (Polish), Queen of All Saints (Puerto Rican, African American), Our Lady of Victory (a mixture of Irish, Italian, and Polish). In the strictly Polish churches, after Vatican II services and confessions were in Polish only. Gone is St. Barbara's. New churches include, Our Lady of Perpetual Help, on Ridge Road, Our Lady of Bistrica Croation Catholic Church on Abbott Road, Queen of Angels, on Warsaw Avenue.

Just as close were the churches of South Buffalo. There were three that I would go to, St. Martin's, St Ambrose, and Holy Family. In addition, there was the Ukrainian Catholic Church where my classmates Maria and Lubomir Ostapoych's father was a priest in the Eastern Rite Catholic Church. Some of my classmates and I would attend mass there occasionally. Long before the Roman Rite Catholic Churches offered bread and wine as Communion, the Eastern Rite Churches were doing so. We thought it cool that you could get wine at mass. They dipped the bread into the wine and served it together.

Holy Thursday and Good Friday

Holy Thursday service celebration service was a re-creation of the Last Supper, where the priest would wash the feet of a selected group of attendees.

Friday was a different service as all the statues in the church were covered in purple cloth. These would remain until the reading of the Gospel describing Christ rising from the dead, on Easter morning. Then all coverings would be removed at once, with Alleluia's being sung. It was a very moving experience. I would sometimes have the duty of uncovering the very large statue of the Blessed Virgin. The statue was located so high up on the Altar, that a pulley system was needed to get the covering off.

Easter service itself was conducted at midnight and would last a good hour and a half. Of course, I slept late each Easter Sunday morning. From Palm Sunday to Easter Sunday, we had to serve for eight straight days of religious ceremonies. Very different from today's liturgy where they do not often use Altar servers.

BERNARD T. MCCANN

Saturday Afternoon Movies

Of course, Lent meant you gave up going to movies. Must have been hard on the owners of the movie theaters. My world had a wonderful movie theater just two blocks from home. It was the Franklin Theater.

This was my childhood theater where I spent Saturday afternoons watching serials such as Superman, Buck Rogers, and cowboys shows galore. Early Tarzan movies starring Johnny Weissmuller, as Tarzan also dominated. I remember seeing "The Boy with the Green Hair" and not shampooing my hair for weeks after that one. I saw the Five Sullivan Brothers there and never forgot it. Superman series was always a special event. There was always a great deal of hooting and hollering.

The theater promoted games and events, such as a Yo-Yo contest sponsored by Duncan. It cost $.12 to get in and candy for a nickel and popcorn for a dime. I would usually get popcorn as my mom gave me a quarter to go to the movies. That left me three cents for "penny candy" at Joudi's on the way home.

Joudi's was a corner grocery store on Electric Avenue and right on my way home from the Franklin Theater. This is where we got eggs, and bread. Milk, of course, was delivered. The elder Mrs. Joudi was the sweetest person. Her daughter, Josephine, would be good friends with my mom. I always felt like I was in a good place when I went to that store. The Penny Candy might have had something to do with that. I was very sad when they sold the store to the Witerski's. They in turn then moved the store to a new location further from our home. I used to play with the two sons of Josephine Joudi Shaw. Today, they are both very prominent lawyers in the Buffalo area, the Shaw Law Firm.

Shoes

Next store to Joudi's was Mr. Jacob's Shoemaker Shop. He also sold shoes as I remember buying shoes from him. He was another of the special neighborhood people. He always had a smile and a good word. Eventually his business would prosper, and he would move his store to Ridge Road.

Speaking of shoes, I must talk about the Buster Brown Shoe Store on Ridge at the head of Colton. They had a machine called the Fluoroscope. This machine was promoted to insure the best possible fit, making for longer-lasting shoes and its advertisers suggested families would not have to buy as many pairs for themselves or their children.

If you were born before 1945 you remember an unusual wooden box – known as a shoe-fitting machine – that once lured thousands of people into shoe stores across the country. In the late 1940's and early 1950's, the shoe-fitting x-ray unit was a common shoe store sales promotional device and nearly every shoe store had one. At their peak 10,000 of these devices were in use in the USA.

The primary part of a shoe-fitting x-ray unit was the fluoroscope which consisted of an x-ray tube mounted near the floor and wholly or partially enclosed in a shielded box and a fluorescent screen. The x-rays penetrated the shoes and feet and then struck the fluorescent light, resulting in an image of each foot.

All we had to do was put on our new shoes and step onto the machine. There were three "portholes" for viewing the x-ray. One for you, one for Mom, and one for the salesperson. In the glowing greenish-yellow light we could see the bones in our feet and the outline of our shoes. When no one was looking at us, we would peak at our feet and think it was great fun.

Fun? These machines emitted dangerous levels of radiation for both customers and clerks. For three decades, millions of children and adults in the United States peered into these machines for an inside view of their toes. The power supply drew seven amps and put out 50,000 volts at 5 milliamps, which generated substantial radiation out of an X-ray tube. The only thing between the customer's feet and the X-ray tube was a .039-inch-thick piece of aluminum.

It was only when shoe store employees began showing signs of severe radiation that people began to question the safety of these devices. The hazards appeared not so much to the occasional shoe store customer as to the salesclerks who ran the machines

In 1957, Pennsylvania became the first state to totally ban the use of the shoe-fitting fluoroscope. The associated hazards eventually put an end to continuous-beam fluoroscopy by untrained operators.

Luckily, we only bought shoes once or twice a year.

My Radio

There was a sales promotion that the good sisters had us participating in to benefit the school. I was in first grade. I do not remember how but I must have sold a large quantity of stuff because I was awarded a small radio. Not the pocket size transistor radios that would come out in the sixties but what they called then a table size radio. That radio would become my lifeline to entertainment.

Each night I would be able to listen to my favorite radio shows right up until it was time for lights out. Especially nice was to be able to stay in bed on Saturday mornings and listen to Big John and Sparky. That was a children's show originating from Cincinnati. Big John was a guy named Jon Arthur. He would do all the voices of the characters on the show, including Sparky. The show started in 1950 and was carried daily over various stations. My only connection was their weekly Saturday show, called "No School Today." The theme song was "Teddy Bear's Picnic," which I can sing all the way through even seventy years later. There was a long running serial called, Captain Jupiter. Sparky would start the show by recounting what happen last week to Captain Jupiter. In between, they would play fairytales and adventure stories that I just loved. The sponsor was Buster Brown Shoes. The famous tag line was "I'm Buster Brown. I live in a shoe. That's my dog Tige. He lives in there too." They still make Buster Brown Shoes but Buster and Tige are no longer pictured inside the shoes.

Bob Barrett

Another visitor to the street was my pal, Robert Barrett, grandson of the people five houses down the street. Every summer Bob would come from California to visit his grandfather and grandmother, along with his older sister Audrey. Bob Buchheit and I would be very excited just knowing they were coming. Betty Buchheit would be friends with Audrey and as I write this so many decades later, they are still friends. Their father was a doctor and would eventually move his practice to Lackawanna. That was just the best thing ever. Bob Barrett, my cousin Bob, Larry Butler, and I would all attend OLV and then Baker Victory together. So many games, adventures and just plain fun we all shared together. The Barrett's would move to South Shore Blvd, a definite step up socially from Colton Avenue. Luckily, he would spend time with his grandparents, so we still had lots of time together beyond school.

One cold spring afternoon, we were all walking home from school. Larry, Bobby, Cousin Bob, and I stopped in front of my house. We were joking around as usual and watching the melting snow cascading down the street next to the curb. Somehow, I do not recall exactly what happened, but Bobby Barrett fell off the curb and broke his arm. I called his dad's office, which luckily was just nearby to tell them we were on our way. We walked him to the office and left him with his dad. We did not see him until school the next day. He had a huge cast on his arm. We all felt so sorry for him. But his great humor got him through the six weeks in the cast and back to normal.

The broken arm did not cause Bob any permanent damage. In fact, he would go on to be one of the best tennis players in the Buffalo area.

Mom's Daily Routine

Thinking about us boys walking home from school together made me think of my mom and her after school routine. She would sometimes leave the high school on Ridge Road and walk to the basilica to make, a visit, as she would call it. There she would pray at a back alter dedicated to the St. Theresa, the Little Flower. I know this because sometimes she would take me with her. Other days I would see her standing on the corner of Crescent and Colton talking with Mrs. Guarino and Mrs. Shea. They would stand there for a long time as Mrs. Shea would walk in a different direction along Crescent to her home on Victory. Mom and Mrs. Guarino lived right next door to each other. I have no idea what they talked about, but I assume it was school. They were such close friends. People today do not seem to have the time or place to stand and talk for such extended periods.

Frances Guarino

While mentioning Frances Guarino, I must explain how she became a surrogate mother to me. After my mom died, she would always be looking out for me. It was not that hard as I spent untold hours in their house, or in their yard or on their front porch. Like my cousin Helen she was a guarding angel hovering unseen, observing things, and making sure I was always OK. No more so than when my dad was hospitalized with a nervous breakdown in my senior year in high school. I was alone with Fran off to graduate school in Ohio, Gramma dying the previous spring and dad in the hospital. Between my cousin Helen and Mrs. Guarino, I lacked for nothing. They fed me, watched out for me and were my mothers. This lasted for over a month.

It was cross country season, so I had to practice each day,

in addition to going visit dad at Buffalo General Hospital. Besides that, regular school stuff, I was also applying to West Point. The day of the entrance exam dad called me early in the morning and told me to get him at the hospital as he was coming home. He was not ready to come home. I had to rush through the exam and then leaving it early to deal with dad at the hospital. It would take him months to get back to normal.

I did not get into West Point. Instead, I was accepted at the Naval Academy. Having no interest in the Navy and having been recruited by West Point, I declined the offer. Just one of those times in life when if you turned left instead of right.

Grandmother Moran

It seemed to me that my grandmother, Margaret Moran, was always around. She would move to Lackawanna from Corning sometime after I was born. Her husband, my grandfather would pass away just before I was born. He died because of falling off a train and having his leg crushed. He was a brakeman on the Erie Railroad.

Grandma would have two rooms on the second floor of our house and had to share the one bathroom. She grew up in Addison, NY just outside of Corning, NY. Her family name was O'Connor. She was the oldest of three sisters. We called them aunt Catherine (my mom was named after her), and Aunt Susie. Her father died at a young age. Grandma was forced by circumstances, to go out into the workforce. She became a servant to a more affluent family. Her two younger sisters would somehow afford to go to college, and both became schoolteachers. I knew very little about her family and only rarely had any interactions.

I have described much of grandma's daily routine elsewhere. She did not venture out too often. When her boys finally settled in Lackawanna, she would spend time with them. I was the center of most of her attention. In my preschool years she was my main caregiver. With dad teaching night school for so long, it was just grandma and me most nights watching TV.

She and dad did not get along. I will not go into why, but it had to do with mom, while she was so sick. They did not talk with each other, ever. They would use me as a conduit. They would each talk to me telling me to tell the other what they wanted. Not a very comfortable way to have a nightly dinner. Grandma would pass away the night of my junior prom. My dad and my uncles did not tell me until after I had gone to a picnic the following day. They did not want to spoil the prom weekend. She is buried in the Corning cemetery for St. Mary's parish along with Grampa Moran.

Grandma was the center of a great small world story. She attended a very small schoolhouse in Addison, NY. She never made it past the eighth grade as she entered the work force as we have stated before. One of grandma's classmates did very well for himself. His name was Thomas Watson, Sr, Chairman and CEO of IBM. Mr. Watson would have a son, Thomas II, who would, in turn, have a son, Thomas III. The third Mr. Watson would have a daughter, Katherine, or Kate as she was known. Grandma would have my mom, Catherine. Mom would in turn have me. I would have a daughter, Kelly. Kelly and Kate would meet as roommates at Brown University. Truly a small world. Kate's grandfather, Thomas II, would give a graduation speech at Kelly and

Kate's graduation. He would also donate thirty-eight million dollars to Brown University that day. I remember his speech well. He said, "Money is like manure, it is no good unless you spread it around."

Yearly Visitors to School

There were visitors to our school each year. The first was the March of Dimes. This was the main charity directed toward curing Polio. At that time, in the late forties and early fifties, Polio was a word that scared everybody, especially in summer. Our parents would not let us swim in crowded pools. It was like an invisible monster lurking under the bed waiting to pounce on you.

The March of Dimes would send cards, with slots in them for dimes, to all the schools. They would get passed out to each student with instructions to save dimes. A dime was a lot of money. You could buy ten baseball cards or two large candy bars. If I recall the cards would be passed out in February just around the time Lent would begin and no candy would be eaten.

The March of Dimes would be a major program sponsored by Franklin Roosevelt, who had polio himself.

The other charity that came around during Lent was the Catholic Charities Drive. This became serious as classes would compete to get the largest donation. We all knew it was a good cause and therefore did not mind the effort. Heaven knew you could not buy candy, so all that loose change would go into a cardboard basket each student would be given. At the appointed time you handed in your basket with your donation. This practice would continue right through high school.

World Events Invade Our House

At breakfast one morning in early March of 1953 dad told Fran and me to be quiet. He was listening to the morning news on the radio. It was reported that Joseph Stalin, the head of the Soviet Union, had died. Dad commented that the world would be a better place. His optimism was well placed but naïve. That news captured the headlines. While some things did change in the Soviet system, the "Cold War" would continue for decades. Little did I know that thirty-eight years later I would stand in front of Joseph Stalin's grave outside the Kremlin. When first buried, Stalin was placed alongside Lenin, in Lenin's tomb. In 1961, during a Soviet period of "de-Stalinization" his body was removed from Lenin's Tomb and buried about three hundred feet away along the Kremlin Wall.

The Paperboy

One visitor to the street that I have neglected was the paperboy. In Buffalo, we had two newspapers per day, a morning and afternoon paper. The morning was the Courier Express and the afternoon was the Buffalo Evening News. Each was delivered to our house. I never knew the Courier delivery person. It arrived before I woke up. The Evening delivery boy was a neighbor, Pat "Slick" O'Neil, a guy in Fran's class. He "hired" me to be his assistant. I only helped on Colton Avenue so I would meet him in the early afternoon after school at the bottom of the street. He would go up one side and I would take the other side. He gave me five cents for that each day. We were both happy with the arrangement.

The papers would be dropped in front of Slick's house all wrapped up. He would unwrap them and put them into his blue, Buffalo Evening News wagon. He would drag that wagon along down Electric and up Colton and over to Victory. Nowadays adults deliver the papers and usually by car. On Fridays, in addition to delivering the paper, Slick would have to collect from people. I never got involved with that and I know Slick did not like having to do it. People were always happy to get their paper but paying for it was something else altogether. I lost track of Slick after he graduated from high school.

First Job

Sometime around fourth grade I started "working" at the basilica. The work involved replacing burnt out vigil candles with fresh new ones in each of the eight stands found throughout the church. I would inspect the stands and replace burned out candles before the 10:30 AM High Mass on Sunday and again on Sunday afternoon. Then I would repeat the task on Tuesday evening and Saturday afternoon. You would get wax on your hands during the process. The pay was $.15 during the week and $.25 on Sundays.

In addition, to the vigil lights, the seven-day candles

had to be changed on Saturday afternoon. With these I only helped, but it required climbing on the back altars. This was a fifty-cent job.

I also conducted tours around the basilica on Sundays. There would usually be anywhere from five to twelve people on each tour. Mind you I am anywhere from nine to twelve years old. Here I am explaining the names of each of the statues. The big hit was always when I showed two of the angels in the painting over the northwest exit as the daughters of the architect, Mr. Emile Ulrich. I was told this but never knew for sure. All I could say was that the two girls (angels) were more life-like than any other angels in the church. Once we had completed a walk around the church, I would take people to Father Baker's Rooms which were displayed in the basement of the church. Today, there is a wonderful museum located in the basement.

From the basement we would take the people across the street to the OLV Infant Home. This is where Father Baker would welcome unwed mothers described before as visitors to our street. As you proceeded down the halls of the Infant Home there were these large windows allowing you to look at the babies in simple cribs. Each child more adorable than the last one. Here is where the tourist would be transfixed. As you went down the hall the children would be older and would top out at four years of age.

Now the one thing about this job was that each tourist assumed I was an orphan. Since my mother had died a year or two earlier, I was a half orphan. So, I never said I was an orphan, but then I never dissuaded the tourist of their beliefs. Invariably, there would be a bill thrust into my hand at the end of the tour. I would make about $10 per tour. That was big money.

What did I do with all that money you may ask? Every cent went right into my savings account at Marine Midland Bank at the head of Victory Avenue. I saved birthday money, bottle return money, and about every nickel, I could get my hands on. By 1961, as I began college, I was able to pay my first semester cost. There was well over a thousand dollars in that account.

One other "job" came along when Robert and I were out in front of his house and a neighbor, Cy O'Reilly asked us to help him unload a truck full of asphalt shingles. He offered us money, so we were at it in no time. It did not take long to realize we had taken on a "real" chore. The packages were heavy and course. We quickly went home to get gloves. After that one experience we avoided Mr. O'Reilly when we saw his truck full of shingles. I do have to say that Cy was one of the nicest people. We all liked him in the neighborhood. He ran his business, called Cycliff Corporation, a roofing and siding operation out of his home at 87 Colton.

At that same address lived Mrs. McGuire, the matriarch of all who lived at that address. She was so sweet to all us kids. She would often ask me to go shopping at the corner store for her. She was always generous. Another of those wonderful people I was so fortunate to have in my life.

Bridges

On the trips to downtown Buffalo, we had to cross the Buffalo River at different points depending on the route dad took. As a very young person certain bridges were more fascinating than others. My favorites were the lift bridges that had to be raised when ships traveled down the river.

Michigan Avenue Bridge was reached by turning off South Park Avenue onto Michigan Avenue. The bridge was built in 1930. I was always happy when dad decided to take the lake route to Lackawanna along Fuhrman Blvd. That meant we would either use the Michigan or Ohio Street bridges. On the Michigan Bridge the deck would lift straight up to heights this little boy could not imagine. While stopped watching the ship float by, we could get a strong aroma coming from the General Mills plant where Cheerios are made. That smell continues even to today.

Then in 1959 Michigan Avenue was closed. A ship had come loose from its moorings and crashed into the bridge. It would be rebuilt and then rehabbed in the seventies and nineties.

Another route choice was to turn onto Louisiana Avenue off South Park. Once over the bridge you would be on Ohio Street. From there you would follow Ohio to just before Tift Park where you would go under the Skyway onto Fuhrman Boulevard. Then on to Ridge Road in Lackawanna. Ships and bridges were exciting to see.

Today the bridges are still in place, but the ships have gone. No more grain or iron ore from the Midwest. Watching all that commercial activity may have been exciting to a little boy but this boy is now an old man and I realize the damage all that activity was doing to the environment. As I crossed each of the bridges over the Buffalo River even a child could see that the river was like a rainbow of multiple colors that water should not have in its makeup. The number of dead fish floating on the water was appalling, as well as, malodourous. With the reduction in the commercial activity the Buffalo River has become a clean, non-smelling waterway. If only our ancestors could have done something to have both commercial activity and clean rivers. Alas, by the time people became aware of the problems it was too late to have both. Buffalo and Lackawanna stand as examples of business interest trumping clean land and water.

Jim's Corner Store

Our neighborhood had several what we call today, "convenience stores." I already mentioned Witerski's. The main go to store for us was Jim's at the corner of Ridge Road and Victory Avenue. That is where dad would send me to get bread or milk, beer, and cigars. Back then a little kid could buy alcohol and tobacco without any questions asked if they knew you. I do not know what the law was at that time. I would get dad his Muriel or Dutch Master cigars and his Iroquois Beer. The deal was that I got to bring all the empty beer bottles (there were no cans then) and keep the deposit which was two cents per bottle. That was a good source of money for me.

Jim, the proprietor, was an older guy. He had a brother who helped with the store. One or the other was always present in the store. They were a fixture on Ridge Road for years. The building is no longer standing. I should not say this, but I think it doubled as a bookie joint. I say this because there were always men standing around inside the store. It is only a guess, but I think I am correct about the gambling.

The Muriel cigars were ten or fifteen cents apiece while Dutch Masters went for twenty-five. Bread was only nineteen cents a loaf. I am not sure what beer went for at that time. I could not buy those things at any of the other "convenience stores."

Another store located on Leo and South Park was Walter Wischer's, later Al's Grocery. The family I remember were the Opelia's. They had a son named Ralph, who was close to my age. This is where we would go if were playing at the Victory Playground. It was a short walk to buy a cool Popsicle or Skippy Cup on a hot summer day. The last time I went to Al's was my graduation day from college. I was commissioned as a 2nd Lt. at the ceremony, so I still had my uniform on when I went to get milk or something. Al was impressed seeing a little kid all grown up.

Niagara Falls

Going back in time once more I want to mention my first trip to Niagara Falls. I was three or four at the time. It was pre-1948 for sure as we drove in Ed O'Hara's car (my dad's best man). The only memory I have is when we approached the American Falls, the roar was so loud to my little ears that I got scared and started to cry. I must have put up quite the fuss because we left for home right away.

This little vignette would take on meaning later in life. The falls would be central to both my brother and me and would be a place of endearment for us both. Fran would attend and graduate from Niagara University in 1960, I would do likewise in 1965. We would both meet our future spouses at NU. Most dates at that time would include a walk to the falls. I have taken two of my grandchildren to see the falls both going to the Cave of the Winds, and they loved it.

It is funny that while in college all I ever did was go and look at the falls. I never had enough money to pay for the

Maid of the Mist ride or the Cave of the Winds tour. But with the grandchildren no expense was too much. I even took my grandson Adam on the Jet Boats at Youngstown NY. It was very expensive, but as Adam said upon exiting the boat, "that was awesome Papa." His sheer joy was worth the price. Going to Niagara Falls always feels like going home to me. It never gets old.

Our "Happy Days"

I am sure that most readers have seen *Happy Days,* the TV series, or at least the reruns of it. Well, in Lackawanna in the 1950's, I lived a sort of Happy Days. The place was called Economou's, and it was found between Lackawanna High School and Father Baker High School, later known as Baker-Victory. Two Greek brothers ran it. One was named Jim; I never knew the other's name. The brothers did not smile very much, and they both acted more like enforcement officers rather than like Arnold (Pat Morita) from *Happy Days.*

It was the place to go for a cherry coke or an orange and water. You met girls or at least you tried to meet girls. I assume the girls tried to meet boys. It was the gathering place. Plenty of smoking went on there also. The jukebox was never silent. The brothers did not allow dancing, and that was a bummer. If they did, they would have expanded their business tenfold.

It was funny how the crowd from the Public School rarely mixed with the crowd from the Catholic School. There were missed opportunities for potential couples to meet. After school was the busiest time as both schools dismissed about the same time. The evenings had a more mixed crowd with adults out for ice cream and teenagers making a rendezvous for a date.

At this time Coke was made in a machine that mixed the coke syrup with the soda. With this mixture and a squirt of cherry you had the perfect Cherry Coke, a real favorite. I can still hear the music and taste the cokes. A dime went a long way when trying to meet up with a girl.

Haircuts

Another Ridge Road establishment that I frequented was Gene the Barber. There comes a time in every little boy's life when he gets his first haircut. I remember mine. My mom took me to Gene the barber who had a shop on Ridge Road across from Lackawanna High School. Gene was Fran's barber and I think my dad's, but I am not sure about that. Gene was a kindly person and would continue cutting my hair till he went out of business. That first day I was scared and curious all at the same time. Mom was also nervous as she worried about how I would react. That barber shop would see me every two or three weeks for years. As a little kid I felt grown up while waiting my turn with all the grown-ups and older kids. Gene was always kind and gentle. He had one other guy in the shop who was taller than Gene. I would sometimes go to him for the haircut. He was also a nice guy. Gene would be just another one of those Lackawanna characters that made up the fabric of our neighborhood. It was a montage of sorts, with little pieces or fragments of people and places fused together in memory to create a childhood filled with mostly great remembrances.

Mike Osborne

One of the best things to happen to me was having the best friend and neighbor Mike Osborne in my life. Mike was three years older than me, but we were very competitive in everything we did from basketball to football to our favorite game, curb ball. This is another example of forties and fifties kids making do with what they had to entertain themselves. We needed no adults, no equipment, except an old tennis ball. Colton was like most streets in the city, in that it had curbs all up and down each side of the street. To play curb ball you had to follow simple rules and have a good technique.

The technique was that you had to stand in the street right next to a curb and throw the tennis ball against the curb so that it flew towards the other side of the street. If you hit the very edge of the top of the curb the ball would take off and fly across the street and over the opposite curb. That would be a home run, if over the opponent's head. It was hard to do.

A strike occurred when you threw the ball against the curb, and it went backwards over the curb. If you did those three times in a row it was a strike out. There was not any way for a base on balls. If you hit the curb and the ball was a grounder and the opposing player caught it, it was an out. If he caught it in the air and a double play was possible it counted as a double play if you caught it, one handed. If the opposing player missed the ground ball it was a single. If the ball went over the opposing curb at a level below the waist of the opposing player, it was a double. Above the waist was a triple. The defending player could put one foot over the curb to reach for a fly ball, but one foot had to stay on the street.

My dad would watch from our front porch and be delighted at how well we played together. We rarely ever got into argument because we both followed the rules and just liked each other too much to ever argue. Mike's grand dad would love to watch us. He would laugh at us and cheer us both. Mr. Ruther was very old, but his eyes sparkled as he watched Mike and me. I sometimes thought we were playing for his amusement more than our own.

Sadly, I moved away and lost contact with Mike. I visited him a few times when I would return to Lackawanna but never stayed in touch until I began drafting this book. Mike and I have now visited and talked for hours about how much fun we had with each other. He did not know it, but he was one of the shapers of my character. Mike was an older teenager who showed by example how to be a good sport, a good son, a good friend, and a good person. Thank you, Mike, you are the best.

Sunday Night Hide and Seek

From an age without computers and video games boys had to make up things to keep busy. On Sunday nights Robert, Larry Butler, Dick Hanley, Dave Guarino, and myself would all meet at my house. We had a wonderful room in the basement that we used as a playroom. It held games, books, an actual working Victrola, Fran's camera equipment, stamp collection, my Lionel train set and much more. That was the only "finished" part of the basement. The rest was dad's work bench area, the old coal bin, the laundry area, and the canned food closet. We would choose one person to be "it." The rest would leave the playroom and hide somewhere in the rest of the basement. Of course, the lights would then be turned off. Whoever was "it" had to then find everybody. The first person found would be the next "it." Soon my grandma would come down with a full bowl of freshly made popcorn. The whole Sunday night experience was great. Being with friends who had known each other from birth and being able to enjoy each other's company was just a great time. The popcorn helped too!

Parks Galore

As a resident of Lackawanna, I was very fortunate to live within two blocks of South Park. The Park would be a magical place for me from my early years. Mom would often get out our Radio Flyer wagon, fill it with lunch, Fran and me and take us to South Park for a picnic. Little did I know from whence the Park came or what a lasting effect it would have on my life.

South Park was part of the City of Buffalo's effort to provide for its citizens places to relax, play and simply enjoy the beauty of nature. Two men had the initial plans developed for Buffalo with designs for eventually six magnificent parks covering north, central, and south Buffalo. Interspersed between and around the parks were a series of parkways and avenues designed to accommodate beautiful homes as residential neighborhoods followed the roadways.

Frederick Law Olmsted and Calvert Vaux conceived and designed this ambitious plan. After winning the right to design Central Park in New York City these two led a movement throughout the United States to create urban oasis for the working class. The Buffalo Parks were conceived in the late 1860's and were mostly completed by the country's centennial in 1876.

The first parks were Delaware, the largest and most used park even today, Humboldt Park, originally conceived as a parade ground, Front Park, which gave a view of the Niagara River and Lake Erie. Later came South Park (1893), with its Botanical Gardens, a small lake and tree lined circular road, and then Cazenovia, with Cazenovia Creek meandering through it. Later, would come Riverside Park in the Black Rock section of Buffalo, with its spectacular views of the Niagara River and the Canadian shore.

On each of the Parkways designed by Olmsted and Vaux rows of majestic elm trees were planted. Even up to the 1950's driving along any of these parkways and avenues was like traveling within a tunnel of leaves. Then disaster hit with the Dutch Elm disease in the late fifties and continuing its destruction of those marvelous trees into the sixties. By the 1970's most of the elms were gone. Parkways looked like naked thoroughfares with all shade eliminated. This was one major flaw in the Olmsted Plan, that of his dependence on one variety of tree. Also lost to Buffalo and Lackawanna about the same time was the mighty Chestnut tree. Oddly, the Chestnut trees still grow in Southern Ontario along the Niagara River.

Back to South Park and its influence on me. One thing not in the Olmsted Plan for South Park was a nine-hole municipal golf course. The course became my go to place to play golf. While still in early grammar school I could not afford the $.50 fee so Mike Osborne and I would get up at five in the morning, rush to the course and be finished by seven-thirty, long before the clubhouse was open. My dad had given me a starter set of clubs, just right for a seven- or eight- year- old. I would use those clubs for years. Eventually, I could afford the greens fee and played using my mom's clubs. I became a regular at the course.

One day stands out in my memory. That day I was playing with one of our neighbors, Tom Merrick, Sr. Tom taught high school with my mom and his wife was the local librarian at the Lackawanna Library. Tom was an avid golfer and a fun person to be around. Well, the par three, fourth hole at South Park requires a drive onto the green over a part of the lake. Getting to that green over the water was a goal of mine for years. This day I hit the green on the drive. Tom, then proceeded to dunk thirteen balls in a row into the water. He was beside himself. He could not believe he was doing so. I eventually talked him into hitting from the ball drop near the green. Tom would be sputtering for the next five holes.

The Merricks

The Merrick family was another of those special Colton Avenue people. They moved to Colton in the mid-fifties. There were three boys, Tom, Jr. a year older than my brother, Mike, who was my brother's age and Andy, two years ahead of me. Mary Ellen would be the youngest. Andy and I would walk home from school together quite often. We would spend hours talking and just enjoying each other's company. Andy would also become a lawyer. He passed away recently just before I write these words. Words are hard to express about this tightly knit family. The parents were both extraordinary principled people. The children were each strong characters, rich in their faith and Irish upbringing.

Speaking of Irish, Lackawanna has the shortest Saint Patrick's Day parade anywhere. At least that was the claim. Tom Sr. would live well into his nineties and for years he would be the official Parade Marshall. The parade would leave the Basilica and travel three hundred feet to The Limestone Tavern where the celebration would continue into the night.

Botanical Gardens

Yes, I know we were in South Park. Besides mom's picnics and my golf, there were the Botanical Gardens. These glass structures, with twin domes highlighting the classic architecture. Mom loved to take us through to see all the variety of flowers, mostly unknown to Lackawanna. The heat that assaulted you was always a surprise along with the strong smell of damp vegetation. I can feel the heat and smell the damp even as I write this paragraph. It has been at least thirty years since I visited the Gardens.

Botanical Gardens of South Park

The Gardens had another use as it sits on an incline that was perfect for sleigh riding. On cold winter days we would trudge the few blocks taking our trusty sleds to that hill. Kids from other neighborhoods would converge on this spot. It made for a nice day to meet different kids to play with.

South Park would also have a nice baseball field where our OLV team played its home games. With practices and games, I spent hours on that diamond.

The most hours I spent at South Park, however, were traveling around the circular road. As a four-year member of the Baker Victory Cross Country team, I traversed that 2.5 mile stretch endless times. Even into adulthood I would go for a run there anytime I was visiting Lackawanna.

It was one park, designed by Olmsted that gave this writer years and years of pleasure, entertainment and sports opportunities and hundreds of wonderful memories. South Park has been giving pleasure to countless thousands of Lackawanna and South Buffalo people for over a hundred years.

Ann Austin

Speaking of the Park makes me think of one of those people that made my world a better place. My mom had a friend and a mentor, named Ann Austin. She was a teacher at Lackawanna High School, like my mom. Ann lived on Nason Parkway, directly next to South Park. I recall mom taking Fran and me to her house on many occasions. Later Ann and her husband Lou, moved to Hamburg NY. The visits continued even there. Ann was like a caring grandmother. When mom died Ann was devastated. She loved my mom so deeply. Dad made sure that we boys would be part of Ann's life for as long as possible. Little did he know that would indeed be a long, long, time.

After Ann's husband Lou died, she would move, remarry and when that husband died, she remarried again but by this time she was in an assisted living arrangement in Amherst NY. During all those years I would occasionally call her or visit. Once I started working in Buffalo on a regular basis, I made a point to see her every time I went to Western New York. At first, I could take her out for rides or dinner but eventually as she aged, she was moved to a regular nursing home. One time she indicated she had a niece in the nursing home and wanted me to meet her. I am thinking the niece worked at the home. But alas, in comes this elderly lady, in a wheelchair. The niece was in her eighties and quite feeble. Ann currently was in her nineties. I had expected someone closer to my age. It was a shock.

Ann was so much older than my mother. Mom was like the child Ann never had. Once my mom died, I became that child. Ann would do anything for me but given her condition she was unable to do anything but tell me stories about my mom. She once told me she wanted to leave me all her estate, but she had given over her estate to the nursing home in return for lifetime residence. She lived in that nursing home for close to twenty-five years. Each time I would visit her she would talk about my mom. She was very sharp right to the end. Those visits would go on for at least ten years. I had asked the nursing home to let me know in case of any emergency or Ann's death. They were kind enough to let me know when she died. I cannot remember circumstances, but I could not make it to Buffalo for the wake and funeral. I felt devastated after all those years of keeping the connection that she and my mom had started. I called my alter ego, my cousin Sue Ellen McCann Duggan to go in my place. Sue, being a Lackawanna school teacher herself, was amazed at all the former teachers at the wake and funeral. Some of my mom's old friends were there to pay homage to this great lady. A sweeter and gentler human you will never find. On one trip while visiting Ann, I was approached by one of the aides, who asked, "Is she your mother?" Ann quickly responded for me and said "yes."

Korean War

There was an international event going on about the time my mom was sick and that was the Korean War or Korean Conflict as they refer to it now. We did not have a television at that time, so all my information came from the radio. I knew what a war was because of all the talk after WWII. I knew it was a faraway place where Americans were fighting something called Communism. That was the extent of my in-depth knowledge. That said, I did know about jet planes. The Americans had a plane called, a Sabre Jet and the Communists had a plane called, a MIG15. Every day, John Cameron Swayze would announce that a certain number of MIGs had been shot down and then a lower number of Sabre Jets had also gone down. I used to keep track in my head about these totals so that way I knew how the war was going, at least in my young mind.

One of our neighbors, Sid Hanley had joined the Air Force and was stationed at Sampson Air Force Base, near Geneva, New York. Dad thought we should stop there on one of our trips to see Sid (Older brother of Dick Hanley). As luck would have it, we stopped at the base. We saw a group of airmen marching right near where we stood. Out of that group came a call, "Hey Kelly." Sure enough, it was Sid. His Sergeant quickly got him back in place. That was all we got to see of him. Dad was happy that we tried, and he told Mrs. Hanley about it when we got home. Neighbors looking out for each other!

In later years I would visit the Korean War Memorial in Washington, DC. While walking around this most moving of monuments I could not help thinking of all those downed Sabre Jets and the men who flew them. I would wonder how many became prisoners of war and were subjected to the Communist "Brainwashing." In a very short time fifty-six thousand American lives were lost and families were crushed with grief much like the Hanley's back in WWII.

To School with Mom

I have mentioned before that I sometimes went to school with my dad when I was pre-school age or on religious holidays when older. But as a very young person I would sometimes go with mom to her school. Nowadays teachers would never dream of such a thing. But the faculty and the administration, especially Principal, Mr. Jack Osborne, were more like a family. They played cards together, golfed together and had a great social life together outside of school. If one day in a hundred someone brought a child to school, it was no big thing. Mom was a business teacher and taught among other things typing. She would not like my hunting and pecking method used to write this book. I would play in the typing lab when it was empty. I would also go to the gym and play with whatever was available. Other teachers would look out for me when mom was busy. The school was one big family.

One school event that I played a major role in was Moving-Up Day in 1948 or 1949. My job was to present a flower to each male student as they crossed the stage. Madonna Smith, daughter of Ed Smith, another teacher, did the presenting to the females. I was wearing a white suit jacket which must have been Fran's First Communion coat. I remember being very nervous. Mom was not on the stage with me, but her friends were there to see me through this ordeal. Mom was so proud of me. She kept reiterating that fact. My grandmother Moran also attended which is something she rarely did.

Madonna was a year older than me. Her sister Joanne would be in my class at OLV. Just three years ago I reconnected with Madonna. The last time I saw her was when we were teenagers. I was on a trip to visit friends in the Washington, DC area, and I posted photos on FB. Madonna saw them and living in the area got in touch through FB. We were able to meet for breakfast the next day. Always a treat to meet old friends but this was special as well as unexpected. She did have sad news for me about her sister who had passed away.

It is funny how people from my era in Lackawanna feel so close to each other. As I have pointed out before it must have something to do with the shared School and Church. With not having seen each other in over sixty years our conversation picked up as if we saw each other yesterday. We have been good at staying connected ever since.

Scouts

One of my earliest memories of my mom was that every week a group of boys would come to the house for a Cub Scout meeting. Fran was a Cub Scout at the time. I always thought it was a neat thing. They did little craft stuff and then had snacks. Unfortunately, by the time I would become a Cub mom had already passed away. I went to Mrs. Sterlace's house just off Electric Avenue. She was very sweet and kind. I enjoyed those meetings. She was a "short-tail relation" as my uncle John McCann was married to a Sterlace. She was his sister-in-law.

I would eventually move up to Boy Scouts and join my brother who was already a big deal in scouts. He was the chief scout in Troop 48. He attained the Eagle Scout Badge at fifteen. I was and am very proud of him and his accomplishments.

The meetings were held in the basement of the basilica. At that time there was a large open area fronted by a temporary altar that looked more like a stage. There were at least five or six Patrols in the Troop. Most were set up by neighborhood so kids who lived near each other could work together.

I had one weekend camping experience at Camp Toad Hollow. I loved the name and still do. There were only memories of the experience. One, was the ghost story that Mr. Turner, the scoutmaster, told after dinner, the first night at the scout camp. He regaled us with a story that I cannot remember, except that as I went to bed, I dug down deep into the sleeping bag. Scary stories keep young kids nervous. Of course, I was not afraid.

The second memorable experience on that trip was on a hike. We had to cross a little stream that had a high embankment. There was an old tree thrown across the stream about five feet in the air. As I proceeded across, never thinking I would fall, I fell. The rest of the hike I was in wet clothes, and I was not enjoying a minute of it.

Sports

Alas, scouting was not for me. I was not into knots, campfires that left you smelling of smoke, and hikes for obvious reasons, nor scary stories. My thing was sports, any kind of sport. I played them all, golf, tennis, baseball, football, hockey, softball, track and field and cross country. Just to compete was my enjoyment. To be honest, I hated to lose but thanks to my dad I was never a sore loser, not that I lost too often. OLV was a great outlet for me, with the great coaches and the bevy of good athletes as teammates. Over the years I have made so many friendships with people I played various sports with and against. The friendships continue to build with my golfing friends. We meet every Monday in season and go somewhere in Northern New York or Eastern Vermont to play eighteen holes and then get something to eat. Great fun, jokes, and companionship.

My love of golf, thanks to dad, would begin at South Shore Country Club (even before South Park) at the age of five. Dad and mom were both members at this club. The owner was a fellow schoolteacher with my parents, Stan Bukaty. Somehow dad was able to take Fran and me on Mondays when the course was closed to the public. We could take our time, as it took more than a few strokes for us to reach the greens. The memory of those days is relived every time I set foot on any golf course. Dad was so patient with both of us.

Dad was a better than average golfer and he did his best to show Fran and me how to play well. From that early start up until dad was in his late sixties, I was never able to beat him. I could hit farther but he hit straighter. He could putt like a champ. He instilled in me a love of the game, which I have passed on to my daughters Casey and Brigid. Casey has now passed that love on to her son Adam and daughter Natalie.

I was sad when I learned that South Shore is no longer a golf course. So many wonderful memories of being with Dad and Fran.

My first set of clubs were a present for my sixth birthday. I used them up to eighth grade. After that I use my dad's clubs until I bought my own set sometime in the early eighties. Dad's clubs were wooden shafts with grips so worn they were perfectly smooth. I loved those clubs and still have them today. Using them was like having my dad along with me.

Ridge Road Businesses

Ridge Road between Center and South Park was the business district for Lackawanna. Colton would be right in the middle of that mix. The Library and Public High School would be on the north side of Ridge Road, near Center Street.

Clustered near Ridge and South Park Avenue would be the City Hall, a loan shop, Bill Osborne's Haberdashery, the Colonial Kitchen Restaurant, a photo shop, Chubb's Jewelry Store, and the South Ridge Coffee shop. On the other side of the street would be Cord's Pharmacy, where I would spend endless hours in the phone booth talking with girlfriends. The front steps of Cords were right on the corner of the two streets. It was also a bus stop for the BTC. There was always someone standing there even if not waiting for a bus. It was one place that reminded me of the Four Lad's 1956 tune, *"Standing on the Corner Watching all the Girls Go By."* Even in Lackawanna, watching the girls go by was a nice occupation.

VISITORS TO MY STREET

This is what we referred to as "The Corner." Ridge and South Park, the center of our life. From, the Lackawanna Historical Association

Niesners' Five and Dime, my store of choice because of monetary limits, was just up the street. Triad's Music store was in that mix. You could "try out" a new forty-five record by going into the sound-proof room and listen to your heart's content. In the early years just after the war there was an A & P located where the Music store would eventually be.

My Cousin Bernard McDonnell

The centerpiece of all this commercial activity was the Lackawanna Hotel. From the perspective a little kid, I only went there for wedding receptions or parties. The first but not the last wedding reception was that of my cousin Bernard McDonnell and his wife Lillian, nee Kilcoyne. Their story is one of lasting, selfless love and devotion. The story of their engagement is worth telling. It was 1945 and the war in Europe was over. Bernard made his way from Czechoslovakia, where he was found when the war ended, to London. From there he put in an overseas call to his sister Helen McDonnell Buchheit. He asked her if she would go to the Kilcoyne house and ask Lillian if she would marry him. Lillian said yes and the wedding above mentioned was the result. My cousin Bernard was, is and will always be my hero. His life was a shining example of what it meant to be a good and loving human being. I was so lucky to have had such an individual be so close to me.

Bernard and Lillian at their wedding reception at the Lackawanna Hotel

Bernard and Lillian would be important factors in my life. After mom died, dad planned with Bernard, so that he would take care of Fran and me if anything happened to him. Dad was also very fond of Lillian. Her dad was a good friend of his. We would visit the Kilcoyne residence often. That is how friends stayed close back then. They would visit each other's homes. Today there would have to be a special occasion to go to someone's home.

After the war, Bernard would start to work at the Westinghouse plant, in Cheektowaga NY, near the Buffalo Airport. We would sometimes visit him at his place of work. He would eventually leave Westinghouse, where he was an engineer. He ended up at Corning Glass Corp. and moved to Elmira NY.

He would retire early but still did consulting work that took him and Lillian all over the world. In retirement they moved to Sun City in Arizona. We visited with him and Lillian on a wonderful trip out west. After Sun City they moved to Oregon to be closer to their daughters Mary and Kathy. Lucky for me I was able to visit him in Oregon over the years. It was always special just talking with him. He would pass away in his late nineties. He was one classy, smart, and handsome guy. More importantly he was a much-respected human being.

Sometime in the mid-eighties Bernie returned to the east coast to attend a military reunion of his World War II outfit. It was being held at the Friar Tuck Inn in the Catskills. He was gracious enough to invite me to join him at the reunion. The unit went to Northern Africa in early 1942 with thousands of engineers. At the reunion were less than thirty veterans or members of veteran families.

As Bernie started introducing me to his fellow veterans, I could not help noticing that every single one of them referred to Bernie as "Sir" or "Colonel." After forty years those men still held him in such high regard, they gave him his war time rank. He started WWII as a 2nd Lt just out of the Penn State ROTC Program.

When the formal meeting was over, Bernie took me to his room where I spent the next four hours listening to him describe his version of WWII. I was mesmerized and amazed.

The story began in North Africa where he was already the unit Executive Officer. A new commander of his unit appeared one day. His name was Lt. Col. Richard "Dick" Arnold. The unit was then conducting mine clearing activities on the beach head. Bernie advised the new commander not to go the beach while the enlisted men were working on the mines. He said officers made the men nervous. Arnold ignored the advice and went to the beach to oversee the work detail. An accident ensued and Arnold was killed instantly by an exploding mine.

At this point I must point out that Lt. Col. Arnold was engaged to a Kay Summersby. For those unfamiliar with Ms. Summersby, she was assigned as General Eisenhower's permanent driver during WWII. Later it was rumored that she was Ike's mistress. Ike's wife Mamie never did join him in Europe during the war. At the time of Arnold's death, Ms. Summersby was working in very close proximity to Ike.

A few days after the accident, Bernie received a call from General "Beetle" Smith, Ike's Chief of Staff. The General was furious. He wanted to know why Headquarters had not been informed of Lt. Col. Arnold's death. Not having a good answer Bernie just listened to a very good chewing out.

The next day General Smith was on the line again, but this time his tone was gratuitous and gentle. Ike found out that Lt. Col. Arnold was still married to Mrs. Arnold, who was back in the states, at the same time he was engaged to Kay Summersby. Kay had written love letters to Arnold and that he kept them with his personal affects. When a soldier died his body, and his personal affects would be placed in a body bag and sealed for shipment home. Ike, not wanting, the now widow, to see those letters, General Smith asked Bernie, if he would retrieve the love letters. Army protocol demanded that once a body bag was sealed it was to remain that way until opened at home in the states. The General assured Bernie that he would have Ike's permission and authority to do anything to get those letters back. Bernie, being the resourceful officer that he was, did not have to use Ike's name to get them back. The letters were delivered to General Smith as requested.

A month later, Ike was in North Africa to review the troops. As Ike and General Smith were walking amongst the rows of soldiers they stopped right in front of Bernie. General Smith introduced Ike to Bernie and reminded Ike about the Officer who retrieved the letters. Ike thanked Bernie profusely. Not every soldier was able to meet the Supreme Allied Commander and future President of the United States.

Bernie would go on to relate how he went from North Africa to Sicily. After a short stint in Sicily, he was called back to England where he would train until D-Day. His account of what it was like to come ashore in the first wave at Omaha Beach had the hairs on my neck standing up.

He would march across Europe till he reached the Rhine River. He was on patrol looking for a suitable place to build a bridge across the river when a German sniper wounded him. He refused to be sent back to the rear. He told me he had been with the same group of guys since North Africa. If he went back to the hospital, he would return to the front with replacement troops. That would raise his risk level of being killed. He stayed in the first-aid tent until able to return to duty. His unit would eventually end up in Czechoslovakia as the war ended.

The medals he was awarded speak to his bravery. I am so proud of my first cousin.

I should note that Bernie was one of five siblings to serve during WWII. His brothers, Joe, Jackie, James, and his sister Kathrine would all see time overseas. My aunt Liz must have been terrified every day. She would have five Blue Stars on her front window to let folks at home know that the McDonnell's were doing their part for the war effort.

The Langans

One of our neighbors, Mrs. Langan worked at Lackawanna Hotel, and I would often see her there. Her son Mike was one of my childhood heroes. He was a handsome guy and a great athlete. He would be the guy, who in a touch football game would throw a long pass to me and I caught it. I was in fourth grade at the time. That one catch pushed me up on the chosen list when sides were being picked for future games. No longer last, I was an upper-tier player from then on. Mike would go on to get his Doctorate and eventually would write two books about his early life in Lackawanna. I am in contact with his sister Bea on FB.

Lawyer Sullivan

In the neighborhood was a lawyer, John Sullivan. He and his wife had a home on Ridge Road between Colton and Victory. My first interaction with them was when I went to my brother's debating team matches. Mr. & Mrs. Sullivan coached the high school debating team. They held the matches in the Old Protectory Building. Fran would take me along sometimes. I was always impressed with their ability to come up with arguments. This was one of my first encounters with the use of language as a tool. It had a profound effect on me. The Sullivans were so nice. They both seemed to know about so many topics.

Years later when I was contemplating going to Law School, I went to Mr. Sullivan for advice. He was so gracious and gave some wonderful advice to a neighborhood kid.

My Bike

I have previously talked about how I learned to ride a 26-inch bike. What I left out was the wonder of the freedom riding a bike can give. At first, my outer limit was the two blocks south of our house. That would get me to Bobby's or Larry Butler's. As I grew older the outer limits would extend to the Victory Playground and as far as Rosary Avenue. The bike was stored in our garage. On Saturdays, my first move was always to get the bike out and prepare to take flight.

The Trip Mom Did Not Get to Take

Two months after mom died dad would take Fran and me to Auriesville, New York. Located along the Mohawk River, was the Shrine of the North American Martyrs, now called the Shrine of Our Lady of the Martyrs. It is a Roman Catholic Shrine dedicated to three Jesuit missionaries who were martyred there and to Saint Kateri Tekakwitha, a Mohawk/Iroquoian woman who was born at Auriesville. Dad and mom always wanted to visit this holy place, but her illness got in the way. We stayed in the Jesuit guest house. The church built there was circular, as Native Americans did not believe in angles. Fran's Boy Scout troop had a camp named after Kateri Tekakwitha. Dad made clay moldings of the image of Kateri Tekakwitha, and we kept some around the house. Visiting her shrine was something important to dad. He was doing it for mom, I am sure.

There were also life size Stations of the Cross that spread along the slope heading towards the Mohawk River. As a little kid I should have been bored but somehow the stories of Native Americans, priest and saints hit a nerve. I would revisit Auriesville three times in later life. It is one of those places you can just feel that something special happened there.

Fran would buy a book from the gift shop on July 9, 1952, as noted by Fran in the front of the book. I still have that book today. It is called *Saints Among Savages, The Life of Isaac Jogues*, by Fr. Francis Talbot, S. J. It was first published in 1935.

That trip would have a profound effect on me. It was our first trip without mom. It must have been very hard on dad as I know he and mom talked about making that trip for some time. Ironically, the parish I belong to today in Chestertown NY is St. Isaac Jogues Parish.

VISITORS TO MY STREET

First Trip to Washington DC

The year after the trip to Auriesville, dad would take Fran and me to Washington DC. I learned only recently that dad and mom went there on their honeymoon. This information came from a newspaper clipping in the Corning newspaper. My cousin Cathy Messner gave it to me. Her dad, my uncle John, had kept it in an old folder. Little did I know in 1953, that I would call Washington DC my home some15 years into the future. (It was just south of DC in Occoquan, VA.)

We, meaning dad, drove all the way from Lackawanna to a northern Virginia town called Woodbridge where we stayed during our DC visit. (This town was right next to Occoquan.) We saw the sights around DC, including Arlington Cemetery. In 1953, there were fewer sights to see. The Smithsonian was the red brick Castle Building on the Mall. I remember the Spirit of St. Louis hanging from the ceiling as you entered the Castle.

One day I do remember quite well, was the visit to the Capitol. There were no security check points and few guards. The one place security was present was at the entrance to the House and Senate. You needed tickets from a congressperson or senator to enter either chamber. Dad refused to go to our congressperson, a guy named John Pillion. Dad could not stand him. We went to the Senate Office Building (In 1953 there was only one Senate Office Building) to see our New York Senators. We somehow were able to take the train that carried senators and staff between the Capitol and the Office Building. That was cool.

As it turned out both of the New York State Senator's offices were closed. Undeterred, dad went into the first office he found open. It happened to be Senator John J. Williams of Delaware. It also just happened that he was the only one in the office. He came out and greeted us as if we were from his state. The guy could not have been nicer. I have never forgotten his kindness. Without batting an eye lash, he produced tickets to enter both the House and the Senate. He also gave us passes to other venues along the Mall. Fran kept one of these as shown below. We were all grateful to the Senator.

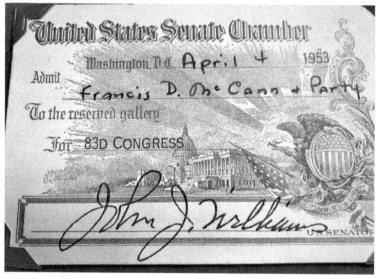

Pass from Senator Williams

While authoring this book I took the time to look up senator Williams. He would serve four six-year terms as Senator. He was known for his integrity and his ability to do the right thing. He would vote his conscience rather than follow his party.

One thing I remember about the Mall was that it still had

buildings occupied by the Naval Department (Until 1947 the Naval Department was a Cabinet level department.) As I understand it, when the pentagon was built during World War 11, the Navy thought they would lose influence, if housed in the same building as the Army. Thus, they refused to go into the Pentagon when it was first opened, choosing instead to remain on the Mall. Those buildings were found just east of where the Vietnam Memorial is today on what is now that Constitutional gardens.

One other site we enjoyed was the Franciscan Monastery, near Catholic University. There they had a mock Catacombs you could walk through. To a little kid that was something different. Of course, I knew all about the Catacombs from religion class. Thinking back dad did a great job of making sure we saw everything. We even traveled to Mount Vernon which I have visited often since 1953. Seeing the home and grounds of George Washington made an impact.

The return trip to Lackawanna would be equally exciting for both Fran and me. Dad would take us to Gettysburg Battlefield. Now in 1953 tourism was not what it is today. The Battlefield was not overrun with tourist. Dad arranged for a Park Ranger to ride in our car and direct us around the Battlefield.

I particularly remember getting out of the car at a place called Devil's Den. Fran and I poked around until I crawled over a rock and came face to face with what I thought was a soldier. It turned out to be a photograph attached to the rock. It sure gave me a fright.

After the tour we spent time in the gift shop. We were

both told we could get one souvenir each. We both found ourselves looking at Civil War hats. Fran bought an Officer's hat and I an enlisted hat. We were both happy with our choices. I did not know the difference until we started playing war at home and he was giving orders.

The one other thing dad bought for us was a long-playing record album. It was from the radio (later TV) show called *You Are There, the Battle of Gettysburg,* narrated by Walter Cronkite. The record took you into the battle with news reports from reporters throughout the battlefield. I can still hear Mr. Cronkite saying, "And now a report from Marvin Kalb on top of Little Round Top." Fran and I would play that record over and over until it started to wear out. I believe we both got our love of history from that trip. I wish still had that record. Thanks, Dad for the great opportunities you gave us.

Lonely Summers

Fran was in eighth grade when mom died. Once he was in high school, he started working summers at the NYC Police Athletic League camps in the Catskills. That meant he was not around for summers of my elementary years. I missed him. He was more than just a brother. We shared so much, including the loss of our mother. It also meant that I was the only one around to cut the grass and clean windows in the summer. Cutting the grass meant using a hand powered mower. Now we did not have a big lawn, so the job did not take long. However, pushing that hand mower around was not easy for a little kid.

The one upside to Fran's employment was that we got to take him and bring him home. That gave dad and I road trips twice a summer. I remember that we stayed in cabins as motels were a new concept and were far and few apart.

My Lost Bike

It was a green and tan Road Master, the kind with a horn on the section from the steering wheel to the seat. I took that thing everywhere till that awful day when I took it to Economou's. When leaving to go home the bike was nowhere to be found. I was devastated, to say the least. Dad was not too happy either. He reported it to the police (the theft took place across the street from the police station.)

The upside was a great lesson that I never forgot. I always lock my car and my house. In later years, I have been the victim of theft only twice. The first time I was an Army Officer at Fort Belvoir, Virginia. I was a Courts and Boards Officer for the Brigade, so I had my own office that I shared with a secretary and two clerks. For our entertainment I brought in a dandy portable radio with AM/FM and Shortwave. It had a nice leather case. One day when coming into work I discovered it was missing and never to be seen again.

The second theft was a home invasion. Someone broke into my home during the workday around 2003. They stole things including a computer, DVDs, and jewelry. That experience left me feeling violated. It is a terrible feeling that someone with ill intent was walking around inside your home. Even my caution from all those years ago could not stop a burglar. He or they gained entrance through a cellar window that had been left open. The police never found the culprits. My USSA insurance paid for all the losses.

After that I became even more vigilant with home and car being locked each night and days when not at home.

At the Old Knights of Columbus

Each year two visitors to the city came to the K of C building on Ridge and Rosary. The first was the annual K of C Carnival. It took place on the grounds around the building which was a very large old house converted into meeting rooms and a bar. This was where I took my first ride on a Ferris wheel and big swing machine. There were games of chance, little kid rides, and a pony ride. I was always excited about the carnival. By the time I was going into high school the carnival was no more. The Knights had moved into new quarters on South Park with not enough land for a carnival.

I do have to say that I had my first ride on a Ferris wheel or any other amusement ride with a girl at this carnival. That is a whole other story not to be covered in this writing.

The other annual event that took place at the K of C was the Christmas Party. Dad always took us. There was a Santa Clause and Mrs. Claus, Christmas caroling and little presents for the kids. I remember the caroling especially because there was one woman with a big voice who always sang Adeste Fideles. She would stand at the top of the main stairway so everyone could see and hear her. Even to this little mind she was very powerful and captivating. Alas, the Christmas party faded into non-existence. Another moment from the past that is no more.

VISITORS TO MY STREET

Who Am I?

As an adult I still appreciate those special places where I can meet myself and delve into my youthful thinking. I suppose it is like meditation but not quite. It is a chance to assess where and who you are. Those early solitary play times provided a basis for my future of self-assessment.

From the time mom died, dad would be a daily visitor to her grave. We would go every night after dinner in the good weather. Dad would take the time to cut flowers and fix the grass around the headstone. Prayer, of course, was a part of our routine but I found that I would just talk with my mom, something I still do all these years later. I do not get back to Lackawanna very often anymore. But when I do, a visit to their joint graves is always first on the agenda. Now I talk to both.

Local library

There is no place, apart from the Basilica, in Lackawanna that means more to me than the Lackawanna Library. Located on Ridge Road just past the old Lackawanna High School. It was built in 1922 with money donated by Andrew Carnegie. It was one of his last public libraries. The building itself was built on the site of a Potter's Field. A monument now stands at the rear of the library honoring the dead buried there.

For me, the beautiful woodwork and the special rooms always made me feel comfortable going to the library. Mom would always make sure I went to the Story Hour. I would love to hear the stories. Ray Albee's sister Shirley was the one who read the stories. My love of reading started in that Children's Room at the Lackawanna Library. Thank you, Shirley for helping to foster that love of books and reading. From the early children's books that I signed out of the library through the intervening years to today, there have been thousands of books with worldwide adventures that have enriched my life. It all started in the Lackawanna Library.

One night during early high school I was writing a research paper in the main floor reading room. I heard a loud noise like a gun shot. I looked up at the window facing Ridge Road. There was a bullet hole in the window. The bullet went over my head and into the wall. I decided it was time to go home. That gave me a scare.

Train Station

Just below the overpass on McKinley Parkway there was a train station. It was part of the Lehigh Valley Line. At one point it was Lackawanna's window to the world. In mid-May 1949, I remember mom and dad taking Fran and me to see the New York State Freedom Train. It was meant to be a strictly New York State version of the National Freedom Train that was sponsored by the National Heritage Foundation as a national traveling exhibit. According to the Freedom Train website, in the heady days after World War II, the American Heritage Foundation sponsored a seven-car train that traveled across all the then forty-eight states, stopping at three hundred plus cities. It was part celebration and part history lesson. It carried many of the country's most historic documents.

The New York State version, according to the New York State Freedom Train website, was a six-car train pulled by a steam engine. Three of the cars had displays of historic interest to New York. Almost a million people took part in visiting the train, people from Lackawanna, included.

There was a second National Freedom train during the Bicentennial Celebration in 1976. I would take all three of my daughters to see the exhibition, which included a Moon Rock.

Chestnut Ridge Park

There is another favorite spot in Western New York that holds untold memories for me and thousands of other Western New Yorkers and that is Chestnut Ridge Park, part of the Erie County Park System. The Park is in Orchard Park and has over 1200 acres and has been part of the County Park system since 1926. There are great toboggan runs. At the top of the hill, you get a view of Downtown Buffalo and the Canadian shoreline beyond. During my adult life, if I were anywhere near Chestnut Ridge, I would go to that spot on the top of the toboggan run and just marvel at the scene. At sunset, you can watch the sun float into Lake Erie, see the sun reflect off the tall buildings of Buffalo and see the dome of OLV Basilica shine. I would absorb all of that as it encompasses the places so cherished from my early life.

Mom and dad would often take Fran and me to have

picnics at any number of the hundreds of places with tables and fire pits throughout the park. Invariably, there would be a swing set or another playground apparatus nearby for us to play on. After mom died, we seldom went, if at all, as a family. However, the OLV Altar Boys would have an annual picnic at Chestnut Ridge. Father LaRusch would rent a bus and cram all of us in for a day of fun at Chestnut Ridge. He was a strict man and a stickler for ceremonial details. Yet, we all knew he was kind and generous to each of us. He would eventually become a Reverend Monsignor and long-time pastor of St. Mary's of the Lake, passing away in 2003. He was one of those visitors to the street that left an indelible mark on my brain. To this day whenever I start a journey or even a short walk, I do so by saying to myself, "*procedomus*," which I thought meant "proceed with God" in Latin. After researching that phrase, I am probably wrong, but let us go with my memory. Father LaRusch would always say this phrase when he wanted us altar servers to leave the sacristy and move with him to the altar. The altar server on the right would ring the sacristy bell so that mass attendees would know the priest was coming. Funny how small things stick in your head and stay with you throughout life.

Later years our family would have birthday parties for my Uncle Tom McCann as we mentioned before.

Other attractions at Chestnut Ridge, for a little boy, were the baseball fields and tennis courts and especially the climb down and up the 100-step staircase taking you to Eighteen Mile Creek. The creek was an adventure found in this ravine where the sun seldom shone. You could walk in the shallow creek bed with its shale bottom and pick up great skipping stones. Skipping stones was a favorite delight, as well as just getting wet. You never went down the steps without counting each one and there were exactly one hundred.

Dad at the Beach

Sometimes just a single day stands out in your mind. For me it was a hot summer day when my dad took Bob and me out to the beach in Evans. The events of that day were by themselves not important but in totality they said much. First, that dad was willing to take the time to drive forty-five minutes one way just so Bob and I could have fun in the water, was remarkable. Dad, in my lifetime never wore a pair of short pants. Only when working in the summer did he even resort to wearing a pair of khaki trousers. He always wore dress pants no matter where he was going. True to form, dad had on dress pants and a collared shirt that day at the beach.

His patience was something else. I can still see him sitting on the blanket with a long sleeve shirt and long pants. He did not have a book or other form of entertainment except to watch Bob and me. We splashed and swam and dunked each other. Dad would just sit watching and enjoying the sight of his son and grandnephew having fun. The sacrifices he made for Fran, and me could never be repaid. Thanks dad.

Travel by Wagon

Another moment in time was the day my mom took Fran and me to the Sears store on Seneca Street. The distance must be about three or four miles. Mom put us both in our wooden wagon and started walking towards South Buffalo. This had to be before we had a car so it must have been 1947. Mom was only thirty-seven at the time, so she was up to that challenge. Fran walked at first, but I seem to remember him taking full advantage of the ride, but I could be wrong. That was the longest ride we ever took with the wagon. I also remember the hustle and bustle of Seneca Street and its shopping area. There were stores and crowds of people. This was a time before shopping malls and plazas.

Speaking of malls and plazas, the first and only plaza in Lackawanna was the L. B. Smith Plaza on Abbott Road. It was named for the Ford car dealership located next to it. By the time the plaza opened we had a car, although it was only about a mile or so from home. The Abbott Theater was just down from the plaza and would replace the Franklin as the place to see movies. It was a bit of a shock at the box office as the admission price for us was fifty cents. Saturday or Sunday afternoons were spent going to the movies and meeting all the new kids from South Buffalo. It is now the fifties, and my world was beginning to open and expand.

Trips to the Dentist

Going back to my early childhood and the start of losing teeth. In the late forties and early fifties fluoride was not a household name, nor had it sparked controversy yet. Tooth decay was common. This little boy had his share early on. My mom would take me to Dr. Ashdown whose office was very close mom's school. I remember his office, the chair, and the instruments quite clearly. He would just take baby teeth out if any sign of decay dared to show its face. My first filling would come later but all I know is, that I did not like going to Dr. Ashdown.

As My World Expanded New Experiences

In my expanded world, which included going to Jim's Corner store on Ridge Road, I discovered a sinister place called Rat's Alley. Mind you it was called that by kids in my age bracket, not necessarily the city fathers. Located behind the buildings on the south side of Ridge between Victory and South Park, it gave easy access to the businesses along that stretch of Ridge. It always had the smell of beer and garbage. Rumor had it that drunks frequented the alley. That never stopped us kids from using it as a short cut to church. Nighttime was especially creepy but always a challenge to be taken up. It was like using the cemetery as a short cut from the Abbott Theater.

If you walk along Ridge Road toward South Park you pass the Old Holy Cross Cemetery. There are no gates on the Ridge Road entrance (at the time that was the only entrance.) Subsequent years saw the end of the Cemetery Pond and the Mud Hole and all the wild fields we used as a playground, as the cemetery expanded and created a second entrance on South Park.

Usually, one of the older kids walking home from the theater would dare us smaller kids to walk with them through the cemetery exiting behind Father Baker High School. I remember the first time I accepted that challenge, I was scared but more scared to show it. The roadways in that cemetery are rarely straight. They twist and turn so that every turn is a new sightline. Older boys would always sneak up ahead and try to scare us by jumping out from behind a gravestone. It worked most times. But alas, we never met any ghost or anyone else for that matter.

War Games

The years after World War II were filled with movies telling the story of the war. *The Five Sullivan Brothers* was a real revelation for us. Stories about Audie Murphy filled us with pride. *To Hell and Back* was a must-see movie in 1955. As young kids we would play at war. One of the silliest games was "who died the best." You would come at each other firing away with your toy guns and then one would be "hit" and would go into death throes. Another kid would judge both antics and declare a winner, to the chagrin of the loser. It was just one of those things we entertained ourselves with. To my knowledge none of us became killers.

Another fun game was a team Water Gun Fight. Teams would disperse and then look for each other. If you got hit with water from the pistols you were out. Last one standing wins.

Other Uses for Baseball Cards

One of the most cherished memories was the gamble of pitching baseball cards. Three or four guys would line up and take turns pitching a card against a wall, usually the school. The card that was closest to the wall would be the winner and he would then collect all the pitched cards. This process would go on during recess and would draw the attention of onlookers, especially when the best player's names were on the cards. When cards were not available then pennies would be used. Sometimes you could be ten cents richer for playing this at noontime. Once in a great while nickels or dimes were used, but this was with older boys only.

Street Coverings Changed our Games

I do not remember the year when Colton went from a light-colored cement covering to a black asphalt. That one event would change any number of games we played in the street. With the cement street there were large rectangles of poured cement. These became boundaries for all sorts of things. The lines were used for "tug of war" games. We played "One Foot" within one such block. It was a form of "tag" where the person who was "it" had to hop on one foot while chasing all the others. The block area was about ten by twenty. It was lots of fun and a few scraped knees. Just one more example of kids having fun without batteries or parental oversight.

Ring-a-Levio

One of my favorite games was a large participant event called Ring-a-Levio. The game, as legend has it, originated in

New York City in the late 1800's. Teams could be as large as you could muster. In our neighborhood, a typical game would have ten to fifteen players on each side. The game is basically a group "hide and seek" with a capture requirement. There would be a circular area designation as the Ring. Captured or discovered opponents would be placed within that ring. The game would continue until all hidden participants were within the ring. The name explains a counter move available to the hiding team. If a player on the hiding team, not yet caught, runs through the Ring, then all occupants are freed, and the game continues. To offset the possibility of someone freeing the occupants of the Ring the seeking team would leave a guard at the Ring. They usually left the youngest kid as guard, which proved not to be so effective. One city block would be the area to which you could hide. Best played after dark. Again, no parental involvement.

Confession

Once you received your First Communion, Confession became a weekly event. As I pointed out before there were five priests hearing confessions at the Basilica from 4 PM till 5:30 PM there would be two lines in front of each confessional with two doors where a penitent on one side would wait while the person on the other side would have their confession heard. It was dark inside. There was a sliding little window the priest would open when it was your turn. Often it was hard to produce so called "sins." I mean how bad could a little kid behave. But produce them we did, and the penance was usually one or two Hail Marys or Our

Fathers. The whole process could take about a half hour, between waiting in line, going to confession, and saying your penance. As you got older this process or sacrament became problematic as the range of temptation became wider. Enough on that subject.

The Plant

For all my time living in Lackawanna, Bethlehem Steel was a major force on the community. From the dust filled windowsills, to the constantly dirty cars, to the rust repellent applied to car bumpers and grills belonging to employees of the plant each winter. It was also the life blood of the economy. In 1965, the plant employed over 25,000 people, me among them. No one could imagine Lackawanna without the plant.

It all started in 1902 when Bethlehem moved its operations from Scranton PA (Scranton is in Lackawanna County PA) to West Seneca, New York. Along with the plant came the workers from Scranton. Dozens of Lackawanna families, including mine, can trace their ancestry to those who migrated from Scranton to Western New York. The Company provided housing just across the highway from the plant.

My grandfather and grandmother and the eleven children lived in what was called the Old Village. That is until 1919, when a violent strike occurred at the plant. My grandfather who had not joined the Union did attend an organizing meeting. The Company somehow got the names of all attendees. He was fired and the family was evicted from their company-housing home.

The Report Card

One of the changes in our society, particularly in education is that young students no longer have handwritten report cards. The drill back when was that on a given day at the end of the quarter or semester your teacher would hand you an envelope with your name on it. Inside would be the handwritten marked grades for each subject and number of days absent or tardy. There would be what they called Deportment evaluations also. Were you a good listener, did you talk in class, were you obedient, and were you tardy or absent? Any adverse grade or remark could land you in big trouble with parents. Today (and this is from personal experience as a teacher and administrator) adverse remarks of grades are generally met with protest from parents.

Once you showed your report card to your parents, one of them would sign the card and you would then return it to your teacher. Some of my fellow students had parents who did not keep up with things such as report cards. Those students would craftily forge a signature and return the card no worse for wear. They were not always successful, as our teachers, usually the nuns, could spot a forgery faster than the FBI. Those so caught were really in trouble.

I never had any worries, as my grades were always high and my deportment exemplary. Yet, one day I was very worried about getting my report card back to school. Dad and I went out for breakfast the morning I planned to return the card. After a tasty breakfast, while walking to the car we passed a mailbox. Dad remembered he had a bill payment to mail. He handed the envelope to me. Somehow, I had my report card in my hand and when I put the bill payment in the box the report card went with it. At once, I knew I did something that was not too smart. My dad had a cooler head. He went to the mailbox and checked when the next pick up was to be made. It turned out to be a fifteen-minute wait. We waited. He explained the situation to the mail carrier and the report card was retrieved.

Not sure there is any moral or meaning to this story, but it is one of my memories of my dad that I cherish.

Memorial Day

In Lackawanna there was always a parade on Memorial Day. In 1952 that would have been Friday May 30th. The parade would go from somewhere on South Park Avenue to The Memorial Field next to the Veteran's Hall on Ridge Road. (Now a ballfield) I did not march in that parade as I was not yet in the Cub Scouts. But I remember that parade because of where it ended. The Memorial Field was also where the May Day parade ended. The May Day parade was the night my mom died. Memories flooded back to me as I stood at the field listening to but not hearing the usual patriotic speeches. I was transported to May first when my mom was still alive. The pain was still raw for me. Since that one time, I marched in parades that ended on that field and the pain would be less each time.

Ice Machine

One of the machines that fascinated me as a young boy, none was better than the Block Ice Machine. The Icehouse was located just south of the west side of Ridge Road Bridge. You would pull up to a loading dock. On the dock was a machine where you would put $.25 in and out would come a large block of ice. These would be used at picnics or large parties at home. The ice made a loud cracking sound as it come down the shoot. Dad always wore gloves when picking up the ice block. I was just always amazed at how the machine worked. Now you get ice in plastic bags from grocery stores. Somehow the bags of ice lack the excitement and charm of those $.25 blocks.

Roller Skating Colton and Victory

One of my favorite childhood activities was roller skating. Not in a rink, although I did that at times later in life, but on the sidewalks of Colton and Victory. As I mentioned early on both, these streets were on a hill for the first block. The skates were the kind you strapped to your shoe and tighten them with a strap around your ankles and a key that tighten the fit around your toes. You wore your skate key around your neck with an old shoelace. If you lost your key, you were out of luck, big time.

This was a springtime activity. As soon as the snow was gone, we would be outside challenging the hill on either street. Now a problem you had to deal with was the cracks along the sidewalk. Sometimes tree roots would make the way uneven. If you were not watchful your skate would hit the raised area and down, you would go. No helmets or knee or elbow pads at that time so scraped knees and cut elbows were frequent occurrences. My knees show telltale signs of damage even today. Scabs on the knee were almost constant.

Despite the danger to our little frames, we would relish the thought of going to the top of the hill and head down as fast as we could, coasting all the way. Stopping was a problem so we would often just lean onto someone's front lawn and fall on the grass. It did not always work, hence the scabs on the knees.

Fireflies

Every year around the first of July the Fireflies would appear at sunset. For little kids this was an exciting time. Out came the glass jars with holes punched in the lids. Each night we would be out in the street trying to catch a Firefly in that jar. You would have to time your move very carefully. You had to catch them in mid-flight and then clamp the lid down and screw it tight. We would take the jar into our bedroom and lay awake watching the magical light glow. We would fall asleep not long after and wake in the morning to find a dead Firefly. We did not equate our capturing and enclosing them to their deaths. No one was trying to be mean, but it was. To this day I look forward to the return of the Fireflies but without putting them in a jar.

Summer Ritual

Caz pool was in Cazenovia Park in South Buffalo. It was a cement pool where kids from all over South Buffalo and Lackawanna would go for swimming and diving. Dad would drop me off and I would be there till he returned later in the day. We had to set times as there was no phone and certainly no cell phones. I really learned to swim at Caz Pool. First you would have to master the side to side, distance. Later you would try the length of the pool. This was hard, not only because of the distance but also the crowds. Caz was always crowded.

There would be days dad would not allow me to go and that was from the fear of catching polio. On hot, humid days he never let me go. It was always a disappointment. The Salk Vaccine could not have come at a better time as I still had years of going to Caz. Eventually, our swimming interest took us to the Lake (Erie) and Evans or Angola Beach.

Dad would often take Robert and me out to Evans and would sit and watch us all day. This beach was right next to the beach that Guarino's used when at their summer residence on Watermen Avenue, Angola.

Gift for Dad one Christmas

I previously said that I saved all my hard-earned money from the jobs I worked. That is not entirely true. There was one Christmas I got it into my head that I had to get a nice present for my father. I had no idea what to get him, but I had five dollars in my pocket, and I was determined to spend it. At that time, the Rosinski Family had two businesses on Ridge Road. One was a large furniture store next to the Marine Midland Bank. The other was a hardware store just past Electric Avenue. I strolled into the Furniture Store with my five dollars in hand looking for something. A nice salesman asked if he could help me. I explained what I wanted to do and what my limitation was. He pointed to a hassock (foot stool) and explained it would help my dad while watching TV and it fit my limitation. I was overjoyed. Looking back, I doubt the price was really five dollars but who was I to question the salesman. I took that thing under my arm and walked the two blocks to my house. I hid it in the garage until Christmas when I wrapped it and presented it to dad. He loved it. That hassock gave him (and me) years of foot and leg relieving pleasure.

Sad Story

As I mentioned before I attended grades 1-12 with orphans from Father Baker's Orphanage. From first grade to third grade, I had a special friend from the Orphanage, his name was Ron Shaw. We sometimes played together at recess and were in the same class each year. One day in Miss Hagel's room Ron started acting strange. It was a basement room with radiators on the wall along the street side of the room. Ron, for reasons of his own, climbed up onto the radiator and would not come down. Miss Hagel tried to get him down. I tried to get him to come down. A few of the kids were laughing, thinking it was all fun and games. Miss Hagel must have known better, as she summoned the principal.

The next thing we knew a couple of large men entered the room and physically grabbed Ron and removed him from the room. That was the last time any of us saw Ron. I suspect he had a mental breakdown. I have wondered all these years what happened to him.

Ron had a brother, also in the orphanage but I cannot remember his name. I do remember he made headlines in the local newspaper when he won the Soapbox Derby in Akron Ohio, the year after Ron disappeared.

How difficult it must have been for all the orphans at Father Baker's. I know that the nuns treated them very well but the pain of being left alone must have hurt. I knew somewhat of that loneliness, but I still had a dad and a home. My heart goes out to all those kids I played with, went to school with and played ball with.

1938 Lackawanna High School Yearbook Faculty List
Retyped for Clarity
THE LACKAWANNAN

Berchams J. Boland	Principal
Leo A. Joyce	Assistant Principal
Edward Gunn	Assistant Principal
Eleanor Anderson	Music Instructor
Anne Austin	Commercial Instructor
Gordon Avery	Physical Education
Thomas Barrett	English Instructor
Bertha S. Bivins	Commercial Head
Julius Boda	English Instructor
Stanley Bukaty	Physical Education
Evelyn Callsen	Latin Instructor
Elinor Carroll	Mathematics Instructor
Robert Carroll	Commercial Instructor
Agnes Cusack	English Instructor
Anne B. Cusack	Librarian
Mary P. Connolly	History Instructor
Clinton C. Couhig	Science Instructor
Ralph J. Cowley	Mathematics Instructor
Florence R. Craig	Mathematics Head
Mary Rita Dietrich	Mathematics and English
Rosina Dietrich	Commercial Instructor
Harry Doherty	History Instructor
Francis E. Downey	History and English
Raymond Gibbons	Mathematics and English
Frances S Guarino	History Instructor
Stanley Gworek	Study Hall Teacher
Lillian Kembat	Physical Education

BERNARD T. MCCANN

Ada B. Long	Domestic Science Instructor
Mary McDonald	English Instructor
Thomas Merrick	Commercial Instructor
Nicolas J. Milano	Social Studies Instructor
Catherine L. McCann	**Commercial Instructor**
Francis McCann	**Industrial Arts Instructor**
Edward F. Moss	Science Instructor
Elizabeth Nash	French Instructor
Anna O'Connor	Librarian
Edna O'Hara	Science Instructor
Edward O'Hara	Mathematics Instructor
Joseph O'Hara	Latin and Economics
John P. Osborne	English Head
Flora Pillion	Science Instructor
John Sabuda	English Instructor
Celestine E. Shea	English Instructor
Victor Smith	Industrial Arts Head
Mary Strahura	Drawing Instructor
John Toole	Commercial Instructor
Mary Turkla	Commercial Instructor
Margaret Turner	Science Instructor
Ethel J. Twist	Drawing Instructor
Margaret E. Twist	Music Instructor
Mary Velebit	Commercial Instructor
Gertrude E. Widmer	Commercial Instructor
Margaret Widmer	Latin Instructor
Arthur Willis	Industrial Arts Instructor
Katherine Yerkovich	Latin Instructor
Mary Yerkovich	French and English
Frank Zurbrick	Social Studies Instructor

This list of all the teachers at LHS has my parents and some of their dearest friends. I want to list them here if only to keep their memory alive. They are all long gone.

Ann Austin, who would give my mother a place to live when she first came to Lackawanna in 1929. Ann would live to be ninety-six.

Gordon Avery would own Avery's Florist on South Park near Ridge.

Tom Barrett, who soon thereafter married Mary Rita Dietrich. (My piano teacher's daughter) They would live across from us on Colton and I would go to school with their children.

Stan Bukaty, good friend of my dad.

Evelyn Callsen, also lived on Colton. Her children are mentioned throughout this book.

Elinor Carroll would become Mrs. Voltz and her children were dear friends of mine.

Bob Carroll, Elinor's brother.

Agnes Cusack and Anne Cusack lived on Victory near to us.

Clinton "Bud" Couhig, a lawyer and friend of Dad's who would get me a summer job at the Erie County Water Authority.

Florence Craig was a dear friend to my mom.

Francis Downey lived on South Park near our neighborhood.

Frances Guarino lived next door to us on Colton and would be like a mother to me after my mom died. Her children Ross, Mary and David are like siblings to me.

Ada Long one of my mother's Club friends.

Tom Merrick, another Colton residents, whose story was previously told.

Elizabeth Nash, soon to be married to John Gormley. She was my mom's best friend. I would stay in touch with her for the rest of her life.

Ed O'Hara was my dad's best friend and the best man at his wedding.

John P. Osbourne, another neighbor from Victory Ave. A great guy.

Celeste Shea, another Victory neighbor. His children were good friends of mine especially Tom and Danny.

Ethel Twist and Margaret Twist were two of mom's favorites.

Gertrude Widmer, my mom's maid of honor.

Margaret Widmer, in my mom's club.

Mary Yerkovich, soon to be Mrs. Shea, another Victory neighbor whose children would all be close friends of mine.

I listed and commented on those special names, as they triggered so many wonderful thoughts, about some great people. Lackawanna High School had lots of great teachers. The students of that era were lucky.

A special visitor to the neighborhood

It was the summer of 1960. I remember going to Lackawanna Stadium one morning because I read about a new team in Buffalo. They were the Buffalo Bills. A friend was trying out for this team. His name was Mike Fitzpatrick, a Timon graduate and a heck of a football player from South Buffalo. Mike did not make the team. He would eventually become an Erie County Legislator for many years. He was also an officer in the Iron Workers' Union. On a visit with him at his legislative office he gave me a tie pin with the Iron Workers' emblem on it. I have kept that all these years. Mike only recently passed away.

That "new" team would go on to capture the spirit of Buffalo and the endearment of the community. I have been a loyal fan all these years. Go Bills!

There were so many people who visited my street and my life. I could never mention them all. With each vignette, I tried to paint a verbal picture of life on Colton Avenue and in Lackawanna in general. We all have different life experiences that shape our future. These stories reflect my experiences. Each person or event had some part in shaping me. I am grateful for the many people from my street and to the visitors who enriched my life.

I want to thank the reader for being a "Visitor to my Street."

Epilogue

Time has dimmed the memories of this special time in my life. It may seem "Pollyannaish" to some readers. If I created a feeling that all things were wonderful in Lackawanna at this time, I apologies. It was the memory of a little boy after all. There were bad things happening on Colton that I now ignore. There were men who drank too much. I am sure many of the Plant workers hated the drudgery of their work. The mothers on the street may have wanted careers of their own. The period just did not allow women the freedom to make such choices. Not every family could afford to take the trips that we took.

Most of the people of my street lived through the Depression, and World War II. Some, like my dad, also lived through World War I, as well. I cannot imagine what effect those experiences had on people. They were lucky to live in such a sheltered environment with the protective influence of the church, symbolized by the Basilica and its bells.

The children of most of my neighbors were lucky to have parents who wanted their children to do better in life than themselves. The parents would sacrifice anything to advance their children. I cannot list them all but there were so many college graduates and others with advanced degrees who grew up on Colton and Victory Avenues. Others would go on the be successful in business.

The children from the neighborhood were the first to experience television, and the last to listen to radio programs. They were the first to enjoy Rock and Roll and the last to appreciate the Big Band Era. They had dances every Friday night and they danced with girls or boys in their arms. There were no fast-food chains. They had a soda shop just like in Happy Days. They played outdoors most of the time. Their childhood neighbors became lifelong friends. They knew being on the phone was a privilege and the conversations were always short because you could not tie up the party line. They wrote letters and were thrilled to receive replies.

Today's children live indoors, glued to electronic devices and games. I doubt they would be able to make up a game like Curb Ball. I would not trade my childhood for anything. It was not perfect by any stretch, but the friendships, and the freedom we experienced made it a great time to live and grow up.

I hope you enjoyed this glimpse of life in the 1940's and 1950's. You can make your own comparison for whatever time you grew up. I am glad you were able to be a "visitor to my street."

Special Thanks

I am indebted to many people for their contributions to this book. I want to thank my brother Fran; without his inspiration I would not have been able to complete this project. Unfortunately, he did not live to see its end.

I am most indebted to my dear wife Kathy, for putting up with me being glued to the computer for hours on end. I also want to thank my children, Kelly, Casey, and Brigid because I really was writing this book for them and my three grandchildren, Jordan, Adam, and Natalie Congel.

I must thank my cousin Betty Buchheit Eagan for her steadfast support and for allowing me to pick her brain for names and events. When she could not remember she turned to Pat Galligan, a former neighbor from Colton. Pat, in her nineties as we write this, who has a wonderful memory, and gave us some interesting stories. She once was my babysitter. Thanks Pat!

Others who helped along the way, my cousin Edward Giblin who would look over early versions and encourage me to continue.

Linda Noone Sharon, Paul Callsen, Peggy Crosta Burke, Mary Alice O'Leary McHale, Sheila Haggerty each supplied information and memories and who were all Colton Avenue neighbors from my childhood. Grateful for the assistance of Lynn Rogers Dziak for the map and photo permission. Thanks to my cousin Sue McCann Duggan who would help confirm my memories. Special thanks to Mike Prescott, who reviewed the first finished draft and made suggestions that improved the work.

November 27, 2021

CPSIA information can be obtained
at www.ICGtesting.com
Printed in the USA
JSHW021129120623
43031JS00001B/57

9 781977 251268